# MODERN SPORTS CARS

# MODERN SPORTS CARS

## MACHINES THAT ARE MADE TO THRILL

**Tom LaPointe**

METRO BOOKS
New York

**METRO BOOKS**
New York

An Imprint of Sterling Publishing
387 Park Avenue South
New York, NY 10016

Publisher: Anastasia Cavouras

Editor: Sarah Burnside

Editorial Assistant: Samantha Warrington

Production: Rohana Yusof

Design: EnvyDesign Ltd.

ISBN: 978-1-4351-1665-8

For information about custom editions, special sales, and premium and corporate purchases, please contact
Sterling Special Sales at 800-805-5489 or specialsales@sterlingpublishing.com.

QUMMSCR

Manufactured in Singapore by Star Standard Industries (Pte) Ltd.

3  5  7  9  10  8  6  4  2

www.sterlingpublishing.com

# Contents

# Introduction

There has never been a better time to buy a sports car. Never before have fast-car fans had such an incredible range of rapid and ravishing machinery to choose from. So there's never been a better time to read about sports cars either, and *Modern Sports Cars* exists to document this extraordinary moment in the history of the fast car.

We've brought together the quickest, most beautiful, most innovative sports cars on the market. If you're lucky enough to be buying one, we hope this book will help you choose from the staggering range of options confronting you. If you're simply an enthusiast, you'll revel in the way all of them look, perform, and make you feel.

The criteria for inclusion in *Modern Sports Cars* were loose, because they had to be. Once, a sports car needed to have two doors, two seats, and come from one of the old sports car superpowers; Italy, Germany, the United Kingdom, or the United States of America. No longer. This book features cars from countries as diverse as Australia and Sweden, and those with almost no indigenous car industry, such as Denmark and Holland.

There are four-door sedans; how could we exclude a car as fast as the Lexus IS F? There are sports cars with two doors but four seats, or just two seats. There are cars with engines in the front, the middle, and the back. Cars with rear-wheel drive and four-wheel drive. Stripped-out, ultra-light road racers and cars with every conceivable convenience. Cars most of us might reasonably buy, and others whose price tags start in seven figures, and are limited only by your imagination and what the craftsmen who make them can do.

There are venerable old marques such as Bentley and Ferrari, brash newcomers like Pagani and Koenigsegg, and famous old names that have been revived with extraordinary new models, such as Spyker and—most dramatically—Bugatti.

**Above:** The Bugatti Veyron 16.4 Grand Sport. At its launch, this was the fastest, strongest, and most expensive car ever produced, with top speeds of more than 253 miles per hour. The car was unveiled at the 2001 Frankfurt Motor Show.

**Left:** The Zenvo ST1 is one of the few production cars in the world with more than 1,000 horsepower and only 15 units are scheduled to be made.

And how would you like your performance produced? By a classic, aristocratic Italian V12 supercar like the Lamborghini Murcielago? With a thunderous US V8 like the Corvette ZR1? In an agile, edgy, six-cylinder sports car like the Lotus Evora? Or a screaming four-pot like Honda's intoxicating—but affordable—S2000? The choice is yours. It's never been greater.

But what about economic uncertainty, global warming, and the oil wells running dry? Don't they threaten to stifle the sports car, and maybe kill it altogether? This moment is like a snapshot. In 20 years' time we might all be trundling around in glorified electric golf carts, and will look back in sorrow for what we've lost. More likely we'll look back and recognize among the cars we've collected here the beginnings of a new trend, typified by the Lotus Evora, towards sports cars that are just as mean, but considerably greener.

And then there's the Tesla Roadster, a high-price, high-performance sports car pioneering emissions-free electric-drive technology, proving that fast-car fans needn't fear the future. We'll say it again; there's never been a better time to buy a sports car. But we believe they will keep getting better.

**Above left:** The Chrysler Dodge Viper SRT10, fourth generation in a legendary series originally conceived at the end of the 1980s.

**Above:** The Tesla Roadster Sport is the first electric-only sports car in the world, an eco-friendly vehicle that can still achieve 60 miles per hour in 3.7 seconds, with a top speed of 125 miles per hour.

**Opposite left to right:** The Nissan GT-R drove enthusiasts into a frenzy while earlier versions remained restricted to Japan. The Maserati GranTurismo S is one of the most well-rounded cars in production, while the Wiesmann takes exclusivity to its limits, with hundreds of interior and exterior combinations to choose from.

# Alfa Romeo 8C Spider—Inspired by the past, engineered for the future

The Alfa Romeo 8C is simply one of the most beautiful cars you can buy. Italian supercars might have developed huge power outputs in recent years, and become more reliable and usable, but they have lost the bewitching beauty of forebears like the Lamborghini Miura and Ferrari Daytona. This Alfa reverses that trend, and it is all the more extraordinary because it comes from a marque until now better known for its compact and mid-size models than hardcore sports cars. The 8C changes that perception.

The 8C draws heavily on the engineering skills of its sister brands, Ferrari and Maserati, producing a car with stunning looks, but performance and handling to match. Breaking from tradition, Alfa Romeo chose to create the vehicle itself in its Centro Stile design studio, rather than turning to a famous Italian design house, such as Pininfarina or Giugiaro, as it might have done in the past.

The two-seat convertible Spider is powered by a front-mounted 4.7 liter V8 engine that sends power to a rear-mounted gearbox operated by Formula 1-style paddle shifters. Its aerodynamics have been honed in a wind tunnel to ensure efficient airflow while maintaining the car's gorgeous looks; what works well in the showroom doesn't always work best on the racetrack. It has a steel chassis combined with ultra-lightweight but expensive carbon-fiber body panels. Finely tuned suspension, massive carbon-ceramic Brembo brakes, and 20-inch wheels give the car precise, balanced handling. Mated to that glorious, sonorous V8, this is a car that goes as well as it looks.

This venerable Italian car company launched the open-top Spider version of the 8C at the 2008 Geneva Auto Show. Like the coupé, the Spider will be limited to a production run of just 500 cars. Parent company Fiat might have taken a risk building a vehicle that rivals—and perhaps even exceeds—the performance, appearance, and price of models from sister brands Ferrari and Maserati. But the gamble has paid off; it has created an instant automotive icon. And wealthy buyers who were considering a Ferrari or Maserati before the Alfa came along will probably simply buy both.

**Above:** The name "Competizione" is a reference to the 1948 6C 2500 Competizione, which competed in Mille Miglia in 1949 and 1950, coming third both times, and won the 1950 Targa Florio.

**Left to right:** The Spider is regarded as one of the most beautiful cars in automotive history. The marked dynamics of the car are highlighted by the horizontal groove that has been built into the hood, while the oversize wheels and the powerful rear fender are intended to accentuate the car's force and highlight the teardrop-shaped fog lights.

# Vehicle Design

The 8C's beauty is its greatest asset, so it would be a pity if the driver—having spent all that money—was stuck in a dull-looking cabin while those outside got to enjoy the best view for free. Alfa has ensured that this isn't the case; this car looks every bit as good inside as it does from outside.

The cockpit is a subtle combination of simplicity and elegance that, as you would expect, exudes fine Italian craftsmanship. The occupants are surrounded by hand-stitched leather accented with aluminum. The deep binnacle houses large, traditional gauges, with simple controls in the center console for the entertainment system and climate control.

When the power-folding top is lowered, trunk space is limited to just five cubic feet of luggage space for those weekend trips along the coast, but, with the top dropped, the noise of that engine means it's a sacrifice worth making.

Composite materials have been used in the dashboard and internal panels to cut weight. The carbon-fiber seats can be adjusted to suit the driver's physique, a feature that was previously only available in racing cars. Alfa Romeo offers a huge range of personalization options; inside you can choose from a vast range of hide colors with your choice of contrasting stitching. This exclusivity extends to the exterior fittings, with almost every detail customizable according to the buyer's exact preference. Given how few will be made, it's very unlikely that two 8Cs will be the same.

**Top:** The bucket seats are upholstered in exclusive Frau flower leather, a weave in which the leather is bound to natural fiber.

**Middle:** The 8C has a five-speed gearbox designed to give superior performance while remaining fluid during gearshift.

**Bottom:** The Transaxle design of the Spider guarantees the best equilibrium in the partitioning of its weight, with propulsion in the rear and gearshift behind.

# Performance

Great looks get a car noticed, but a great drivetrain and sharp handling are what really matter to the driver, and make a pretty sports car truly world-class. With Ferrari technology under the hood, the 8C could hardly fail to impress.

The front-mounted 4.7-liter aluminum V8 (8C references eight cylinders) with variable valve timing pumps out 450 horsepower and 354 pound-feet of torque, enough to propel it to 60 miles per hour in about 4.5 seconds.

Power is transferred to the rear F1-style six-speed transaxle through a torque tube for structural rigidity, with a limited-slip differential for traction and instant, on-demand powerslides. Weight distribution is nearly even at 49 percent front and 51 percent rear, giving the car balanced handling. And it offers racetrack-standard stopping power with fade-free carbon-ceramic brakes measuring a massive 14.2 inches at the front and 13 inches at the back.

## At a Glance

**Country of manufacture**
Italy

**Engine**
Front-mounted aluminum engine with dual overhead cams and four valves per cylinder.

| | |
|---|---|
| Displacement | 4.7 liters |
| Horsepower | 450 @ 7,000 rpm |
| Torque | 354 lb-ft @ 4,750 rpm |

**Drivetrain**
6-speed rear transaxle with automatic clutch controlled by steering wheel paddles, and a limited-slip differential.

**Suspension, handling, & braking**
Aluminum double-wishbone, carbon-ceramic brakes.

**Weights and measurements**

| | |
|---|---|
| Curb weight (est.) | 3,600 lbs |
| Wheelbase | 103.5 in |
| Length | 172 in |
| Width | 74.6 in |
| Track F/R | 62.6/62.6 in |

**Performance**

| | |
|---|---|
| 0–60 mph (est.) | 4.4 sec |
| 0–100 mph (est.) | 9.6 sec |
| Lateral grip (est.) | 1g |
| Top speed (est.) | 180 mph |

**Trivia**

The name of the car resurrects a classic Alfa Romeo nameplate.

The Competizione replaces the parking brake lever and gearshift with push buttons.

## Ascari KZ1R—The British storm the supercar world

Extreme rarity and a clear racing link can each make a sports car hugely desirable, and the Ascari KZ1R Limited Edition offers both. The production run is limited to a mere 50 vehicles, which guarantees there will only ever be one on show in the valet lot. It is named for the legendary two-time champion Formula 1 driver, Alberto Ascari. And it is handmade in Banbury, England, at the heart of the country's huge Formula 1 industry.

The car itself is basically a street-legal version of Ascari's A10 racing prototype, itself a race version of the 'regular' KZ1 supercar introduced in 2003. This tiny, privately owned British carmaker chose the legendary Goodwood Festival of Speed to unveil the KZ1R Limited Edition, doing so a decade after it launched its first vehicle in 1998.

Ascari combines space-age construction with engines sourced from BMW to produce cars with blistering performance that match or exceed the established exotic brands. The KZ names reference Klaas Zwart, a Dutch businessman and racing driver who bought Ascari soon after it launched its first production vehicle.

The ability of the Ascari KZ1R to hit 60 miles per hour in the three-second range combined with a top speed of 200 miles per hour puts it squarely in supercar territory. The car is built around a lightweight carbon-fiber chassis that keeps curb weight under 3,000 pounds, and takes eight months to construct.

A front splitter, rear wing, and ground effects make the car easy to distinguish from a standard KZ1—not that you're likely to see two on the road at the same time—and its spartan interior includes an integrated roll bar for track use. Unlike many sports car manufacturers, Ascari has earned credibility with a successful racing program that includes entries in the 24 Hours of Le Mans and 12 Hours of Sebring victories and podium finishes at the highest level of European sports car racing. This car takes that experience and puts it on the road with minimum dilution; question is, can you handle it?

**Above:** Stylish and edgy, built to order at Ascari's state-of-the-art production facility in Banbury, England, the KZ1R is sleek and aerodynamic with a body shell weighing just 2,976lbs and a super-light, super-strong carbon-fiber monocoque chasis.

**Left to right:** The interior of the car has been stripped down to its bare bones to reduce weight and accommodate the integral roll cage, allowing the car to build up to 60 miles per hour in just 3.0 seconds, making it one of the fastest sports cars currently on the market.

# Vehicle Design

Like the rest of the car, the interior of the Ascari KZ1R is meticulously fabricated by hand in Ascari's state-of-the-art design and production facility. While the standard KZ1 has luxury appointments, the interior of the R is that of a barely-softened racecar.

The car's finishing touches include a front splitter and fixed rear wing, intended to turn it from a mere supercar into a track superstar.

Carbon-fiber and billet aluminum dominate the cabin. Racecar details include the Sparco racing seats, a racing steering wheel, and floor-hinged pedals.

The designers passed on a traditional instrument gauge layout, instead opting for a flat screen atop the steering column; again, just as you'd find in racecar and allowing the driver to customize the information he's receiving.

The Limited Edition adds leather trim, power windows, remote central locking, and a climate control system, but don't think the KZ1R has gone soft. Some may feel the interior isn't up to the standard of brands such as Aston Martin and Ferrari, whose badges carry more cachet and whose cars carry similar pricetags. But this Ascari is a very different proposition; it's a hardcore road-racer, and owners won't notice the quality of the leather in the cabin when they're lapping Lamborghinis on the track.

**Top:** The KZ1R has been designed with aerodynamics firmly in mind, with the lightest of body shells and stripped interior.

**Middle:** Built for speed, the car stunned onlookers at its UK debut, where it was driven by Nicholas Cowell, who described it as having 'amazingly precise handling.'

**Bottom:** The front splitter is a finishing touch that turns the KZ1R into the most fearsome of racetrack competitors.

# Performance

It takes prodigious power effectively put down on the track to run with the traditional supercar brands, and the KZ1R is up to the fight. Ascari settled on BMW power, as McLaren did with its sublime F1; BMW makes some of the world's finest engines but doesn't make a supercar of its own; it's fascinating to see a Munich engine unleashed in a lightweight extreme sports car.

The 90-degree, five-liter engine, sourced from BMW's M5 and Z8, has been tuned to put out 520 horsepower and 276 pound-feet of torque. The naturally aspirated, mid-mounted engine transfers all this power to the rear wheels through a six-speed manual transmission. Double-wishbone suspension front and rear, combined with coil springs, have been specially tuned for racetrack performance in the KZ1R, with cross-drilled and vented brakes to rein in the power.

The result is a very different type of performance; harder, faster, less compromised, but less comfortable too. Some drivers will love it, and others will prefer something a little less intimidating. Which camp do you fall into?

## At a Glance

**Country of manufacture**
United Kingdom

**Engine**
Rear mid-mounted, fuel injected, naturally aspirated 90-degree V8 sourced from BMW with dual overhead cams and four valves per cylinder.

| | |
|---|---|
| Displacement | 5.0 liters |
| Horsepower | 520 @ 7250 rpm |
| Torque | 276 lb-ft @ 3500 rpm |

**Drivetrain**
6-speed manual transaxle

**Suspension, handling, & braking**
Front and rear double wishbones with coil springs over dampers. Cross-drilled and vented disc brakes.

**Weights and measurements**

| | |
|---|---|
| Curb weight | 2,976 lbs |
| Wheelbase | 103.8 in |
| Track F/R | 61.8/58.1 in |
| Length | 169.3 in |
| Width | 72.9 in |
| Height | 44.8 in |

**Performance**

| | |
|---|---|
| 0–60 mph (mfr est.) | 3.0 sec |
| Top speed | 200 mph |

**Trivia**
Nicholas Cowell, brother of *American Idol* judge, Simon Cowell, drove a KZ1R at the opening of Bull Run Ibiza, also the British launch of the vehicle. The enhancements to the 'Limited Edition' vehicle add about 200 pounds over a regular production KZ1R.

# Aston Martin DBS—Continuing the Bond tradition

For nearly half a century, an Aston Martin has been the rapid and refined car of choice for superspy James Bond, from the DB5's role in *Goldfinger* (1964), to the two-time appearance of this top-of-the-range DBS in *Casino Royale* (2006) and *Quantum of Solace* (2008).

Bond actually drove a Bentley in the original Ian Fleming novels, and he has flirted with other brands since he took delivery of that first DB5. But the DBS is one of the greatest Bond cars ever. Like Daniel Craig's 007, it's more realistic and believable, with fewer far-fetched gadgets; the car he drives and the car you can buy are almost the same.

But although the bond with Bond is now almost unbreakable, Aston Martin doesn't rely on one of the world's best product placements to make its cars desirable. The DBS easily manages that on its own. Launched at the end of the Vanquish production run, the 510-horsepower DBS isn't a direct replacement, being closely based on the DB9 but sold at about a 60 percent price premium. It's now Aston's current range-topper and carries the brand's colors with honor.

Its hard, masculine lines and aggressive aerodynamic accents reflect that much of its technology was bred racing in Europe and the United States. The racing version—the DBR9—fought for wins at venues such as LeMans and Sebring in the face of furious competition from the seasoned Corvette teams. What was learned has been incorporated into the DBS. According to Aston Martin CEO and seasoned racer Dr. Ulrich Bez, it offers racecar excitement without compromising comfort. 'The DBS delivers the complete driving experience and bridges the gap between our road and track cars—the DB9 and DBR9,' he explains.

Once the six-liter V12 rumbles to life, it can sprint to 60 miles per hour in the four-second range, while its lightweight chassis is a tour-de-force of technology. Copious use of aluminum, Kevlar, and carbon-fiber keep it down, but at 3,737 pounds it's more of a grand tourer than a lightweight track-day car. But we wouldn't want to see James Bond pull up at the casino looking flustered and uncomfortable; Aston Martin's famous client demands power, but refinement too.

**Above:** The Aston Martin DBS has been designed for pure performance, as at home on a twisting mountain circuit as the open road—described by the manufacturer as a thoroughbred, the car combines technology, race-derived materials and components, and the grand Aston Martin tradition of hand-building.

**Left to right:** The body features extruded aluminum, magnesium alloy, and carbon-fiber composite, with extruded aluminum door side-impact beams, halogen projector headlamps, LED rear lamps and side repeaters, and a bonded aluminum VH structure.

# Vehicle Design

The interior of the DBS could easily be the collaborative effort of an avant-garde jeweler and a racecar engineer. It features a unique crystal key fob, referred to as an "Emotion Control Unit", that owners plug into a special dock in the center of the dashboard to activate the ignition.

And that's not all: for the price of a mid-size SUV, Bond fans can order a watch co-engineered with premium watchmaker, Jaeger-LeCoultre, that incorporates a remote keyless entry system. Owners may not be able to fire missiles from their Aston Martin, but they will be able to open it from the wrist.

Once inside, the Bang & Olufsen sound system features front speakers that rise theatrically from the dashboard and offer extraordinary volume and clarity; necessary if you're going to hear your Bond theme-tune compilation over the deafening metallic howl of the exhausts.

The extensive use of carbon-fiber, aluminum, and the fireproof, suede-like Alcantara fabric reflects the racing roots of the DBS, and stiff, ultra-lightweight race seats are an option. That V12 engine can be ordered with either a six-speed manual gearbox or a six-speed automatic with F1-style paddle shifters giving full manual control; power goes to the rear wheels via an alloy torque tube with carbon-fiber propeller shaft and a limited-slip differential.

**Top:** The engine is fired by pressing the Emotion Control Unit (ECU), which is flush with the surface of the starter button. Once pressed a second time, to stop the engine, the unit automatically motors out of the dashboard so it can be removed.

**Middle:** Almost every aspect of the DBS interior is customizable, including the carpets, bindings, facia, and seat belts.

**Bottom:** The DBS interior has been designed to combine function and comfort, with all the tactile rewards of excellent craftsmanship using modern, lightweight materials.

# Performance

Like Aston Martin sports cars of old, the DBS shares its engine with its racing brethren and has massive acceleration on tap throughout the rev range with its 510 horsepower and 420 pound-feet of torque. You'll reach 60mph in just over four seconds and, like other top-end sports cars, you'll need a derestricted German autobahn to fully exploit the 191 mph top speed. Though the company is now independent and owned by a consortium of investors, the 48-valve all-alloy engine with dual overhead cams was developed under Ford ownership. The powerplants are still hand-assembled in Cologne, Germany, in a special Ford facility, before being shipped to Aston Martin's factory in the English Midlands.

The standard carbon-ceramic brakes decelerate the DBS as impressively as it accelerates; on both road and track you can use more of its massive performance knowing that it will stop so quickly. The front and rear double-wishbone suspension, along with the active damping system, keep the DBS composed even when driving hard, but manage to deliver a far smoother ride than the first DB9s. Like Bond, it seems to be good at everything.

## At a Glance

**Country of manufacture**
United Kingdom

**Engine**
All-alloy front mid-mounted V12 with dual overhead cams, four valves per cylinder, and active exhaust bypass valves.

| | |
|---|---|
| Displacement | 6.0 liter |
| Horsepower | 510 @ 6,500 rpm |
| Torque | 420 lb-ft @ 5,750 rpm |

**Drivetrain**
Rear mid-mounted 6-speed manual gearbox with limited-slip differential or optional 6-speed Touchtronic automatic transmission.

**Suspension, handling, & braking**
Front and rear Independent double wishbones with coil spring; front and rear vented carbon-ceramic antilock brakes with six-piston front calipers and four piston rear calipers; traction control; adaptive damping and stability control with track mode.

**Weights and measurements**

| | |
|---|---|
| Curb weight | 3,737 lbs |
| Wheelbase | 107.9 in |
| Length | 185.9 in |
| Width | 81.1 in |
| Height | 50.4 in |

**Performance**

| | |
|---|---|
| 0–60 mph (mfr est.) | 4.2 sec |
| Top speed (mfr est.) | 191 mph |

**Trivia**
The Aston Martin DBS earned automotive awards in three countries: Germany, the United Kingdom, and Japan.

## Audi R8 5.2 FSI V10—The powerhouse built for the racing world

The Audi R8 shocked the sports car world. Famous firms like Ferrari and Porsche have spent decades perfecting their supercars but, at its very first attempt, Audi produced a world-beater; a car with the performance and handling of the very best exotic sports cars, but all the quality and refinement and intelligent design of the company's standard range.

Nobody expected it to be so good. Until the R8, sporty Audis were known for their powerful, characterful engines but often uninvolving handling. This car proved an Audi could do it all, marrying ferocious performance to sublime handling. A new star was born.

Over the course of almost a decade, Audi's Le Mans racers dominated on the track, and it launched the R8 sports car to honor that success. The vehicle debuted in 2003 as the Quattro concept car and was launched three years later at the Paris Auto Show, to great acclaim.

Originally, the R8 featured a V8 engine, but the addition of the V10 has promoted a car that originally competed with the Porsche 911, moving it into the domain of Ferrari and Audi's corporate cousin, Lamborghini.

A curb weight of more than 3,500 pounds makes the car chunky compared to others in the segment, but the V10 will still hit the 60 mph mark in less than four seconds. The optional carbon-fiber sideblade is its most distinctive feature, and this is the first production vehicle with LEDs for all exterior lighting, including an optional set of lights that illuminate that magnificent mid-mounted engine. It deserves the attention.

**Above:** The extra power from the V10 powerplant gives the R8 V10 the boost that its chassis was designed to exploit, with plenty of torque and flexibility for road driving as well as days out on the racetrack—control that's combined with impressive levels of power.

**Left to right:** The 5.2-liter FSI V10 petrol engine, which is mounted longitudinally behind the cockpit, is almost identical to the one that powers the recently announced R8 LMS, which will race at customer level in the GT3 class.

# Vehicle Design

Audi is one of the best manufacturers in the business when it comes to interior design and build quality, and naturally the hero of its range is no exception. The purposeful yet luxurious feel of the interior is created partly with the materials chosen to construct it; lightweight, hi-tech carbon-fiber, the suede-like Alcantara race fabric, but also luxurious Nappa leather.

There is more personal space than many of its competitors; Audi claims there is enough room for two golf bags. Other features include a rear parking system with an integrated backup camera, DVD satellite navigation, and a 465-watt Bang & Olufsen audio system.

The company refers to the wide arc that contains the instruments and the steering wheel as the "monoposto", because it is focused around the driver in the same way as a single-seat racing car. The race-style steering wheel has a flat bottom for ease of entry.

The ten-cylinder engine has been mounted as close as possible to the center of the car to achieve an almost-perfect handling balance. Audi has improved it further with dry-sump engine lubrication, which enables the V10 to be mounted closer to the road, thus lowering the center of gravity.

The upgrade from the V8 substantially increases the R8's power from 420 horsepower and 317 pound-feet of torque to 520 and 490, respectively, with a weight penalty of less than 70lbs.

**Top:** The gearshift has been designed to be fast-reacting, with communicative steering.

**Middle:** The 19-inch '10-spoke Y design' alloy wheels add to performance with the addition of the quattro permanent four-wheel-drive system, dividing power between the front and rear axles depending on the condition of the road.

**Bottom:** Seating for the driver is enhanced by electric adjustment and heating, as well as by the fine Nappa leather-upholstered sports seats.

# Performance

The heart of the R8 5.2 FSI V10 is its mid-mounted engine, constructed of lightweight aluminum alloy with 90-degree cylinder banks. The FSI designation in the name refers to "fuel stratified injection", Audi's nomenclature for gasoline direct injection, pioneered in its all-conquering Le Mans racecars. The revolutionary process involves injecting a highly atomized fuel and air mixture directly into the cylinder, resulting in more efficient combustion. By varying the injection timing based on power requirements, the system can produce more power with less fuel.

The R8's horsepower is transferred to all four wheels via a standard six-speed manual gearbox, or the optional twin-clutch sequential manual gearbox, which offers incredibly rapid manual shifts and a seamless automatic mode for town use. On an open road, a launch-control system balances power and traction perfectly to propel the R8 to 60 miles per hour in less than four seconds. Carbon-ceramic brakes are optional, and the suspension system features shocks with magnetized fluid that adjust their dampening rates for optimum comfort and performance. It's challenging, cutting-edge stuff, but that's how Audi has made this car so good.

## At a Glance

**Country of manufacture**
Germany

**Engine**
90-degree direct-injected rear-mid V10, with dry-sump lubrication and 90-degree cylinder banks for a low center of gravity; four chain-driven camshafts.

| | |
|---|---|
| Displacement | 5.2 liter |
| Horsepower | 525 @ 8,000 rpm |
| Torque | 520 lb-ft @ 6,500 rpm |
| Redline | 8,700 rpm |

**Drivetrain**
Manual 6-speed rear transaxle or optional 6-speed sequential R tronic; launch control mode for both transmissions; all-wheel-drive system that defaults to 90 percent of torque to the rear wheels with viscous coupling center differential.

**Suspension, handling, & braking**
Front and rear independent double wishbones with coil spring; front and rear antilock drilled and ventilated brakes with eight-piston front calipers and four piston rear calipers (carbon-ceramic optional).

**Weights and measurements**

| | |
|---|---|
| Curb weight | 3,571 lbs |
| Wheelbase | 104.4 in |
| Length | 174.6 in |
| Height | 49.3 in |
| Weight distribution | 44/56 |

**Performance**

| | |
|---|---|
| 0–62 (mfr est.) | 3.9 sec |
| Top speed (mfr est.) | 196 mph |
| Lateral acceleration | 1.2g |

# Bentley Continental GTC Speed—The muscle car with luxury appeal

The Bentley Continental GT coupé transformed the fortunes of this blue-blooded British carmaker. Here was a car with colossal performance and an image to rival the most exclusive Italian brands, which could carry four people and all their luggage, and deploy all its power safely and securely even in the worst weather conditions with its four-wheel-drive system. Most Bentley buyers have a stable of other cars but, if they had to, they could use the Bentley alone.

After buying the Bentley brand in the late 1990s, Volkswagen quickly got to work recreating its image. Gone was the stodgy styling and questionable reliability that had plagued the brand for decades. The modern Bentley was not only a technological tour-de-force, but recaptured the sporting character and world-beating performance that W.O. Bentley intended when he started the company nearly a century ago.

Bentley's early dominance in the automotive industry stemmed from its success in racing, and even in the modern era, a brand's racing pedigree contributes substantially to its image. Bentley borrowed some of its Volkswagen stablemate Audi's racecar technology for a return to Le Mans, where it had etched its name into racing history with four consecutive victories in the famed 24-hour race from 1927 to 1930. The modern-day "Bentley Boys" carried on the tradition with an overall win in 2003 with the Bentley Speed 8.

Following the success of the coupé, Bentley launched the convertible, or GTC, at the New York Auto Show in 2006. The folding soft top version was a mechanical twin to the coupé, giving buyers top-down motoring with the same opulence and performance. The "Speed" moniker for the racecar was reprised from early Bentleys, and the company subsequently used it to designate the high-performance version of its road cars. In Speed form, the GTC becomes the most powerful convertible Bentley has ever built, with a staggering 600 hp.

**Above:** The lowered ride height of the GTC speed enriches the driving experience, enhanced by the Sport mode on ESP, turning this model into the most powerful Bentley convertible ever produced.

**Left to right:** The Continental GTC Speed has been designed with a dark chrome grille, 20-inch multi-spoke wheels, and twin rifled sports tail pipes. Bentley claims to have improved the body control, handling dynamics, and grip, and upped the aerodynamics with the addition of the new rear fixed spoiler.

# Vehicle Design

The design objective for the Continental was to create a sleek, contemporary, ultra-luxury vehicle that honored the marque's past. This task fell to Bentley Design Director Dirk van Braeckel. 'My vision for Bentley was to create the ultimate in desirability—a classic of the future,' said Belgian-born van Braeckel, after receiving the prestigious European Automotive Design Award for his work.

The look of the convertible with its thick, insulating, three-layer hood in place may not be quite as attractive as the coupé's, but the car is stunning with the top tucked away. Dr Franz-Josef Paefgen, Bentley Chairman and CEO, described the GTC as "the most distinctive new Bentley yet."

Visual enhancements for the "Speed" edition include dark chrome radiator and lower air intake grilles, 20-inch wheels, lowered suspension, wider twin tailpipes, and a more aggressive spoiler. Interior cues include special insignia, diamond-quilted hides, knurled chrome accents, and drilled alloy pedals.

Despite its hi-tech engineering, it's still the hand-crafted interior that really marks a Bentley out from other high-end luxury sports cars. The craftsmen at Bentley's factory in Crewe, England—once shared with Rolls-Royce—are extraordinarily skilled, and create cabins with the finest woods and leathers that look, feel, and smell like an upper-class English gentleman's club. Customers can even define how tightly-knotted the pattern of their wood veneers should be, and the Bentley's woodworkers spend hours matching veneer panels to give each cabin a consistent look. The Mulliner department takes on the really unusual requests, hand-building from scratch almost anything a customer requests—at a price.

**Top:** Traditional Bentley features, such as the bulls-eye vents, are framed by the wood veneers and premium-grade leather hide.

**Middle:** The standard range of 17 exterior colours is available, as well as a bespoke paint match service for the exterior.

**Bottom:** It takes two weeks to prepare the wood for the Continental's interior, during which the veneers are given five coats of lacquer and three days of curing time before they are wax polished by hand.

# Performance

Volkswagen engineers opted for their unique W12 engine for the Bentley. With twin low-inertia turbochargers, the front-mounted package puts out 600 horsepower (against "just" 552hp in standard guise) and 553 pound-feet of torque. This is enough power to propel the GTC Speed to 200 mph, giving it membership of a very exclusive club. Despite a massive 5,478lb curb weight, it rocks to 60 mph in just 4.5 seconds. A silky-smooth six-speed ZF automatic transmission is strong enough to handle and transmit the power to the all-wheel-drive system via a central Torsen differential. It can be used in automatic mode or shifted manually using the shift lever or shift paddles.

A full complement of electronic systems help manage the prodigious power, and optional carbon-ceramic brakes help stop this sports car that weighs as much as a full-size SUV. Fuel consumption is pretty terrifying, especially if you use all that performance, but Bentley buyers are unlikely to be bothered. And whatever it costs, it's worth it.

## At a Glance

**Country of manufacture**
England

**Engine**
Front-mounted W12 configuration with four banks of three cylinders, alloy block and heads, twin low-inertia turbochargers, four camshafts, and 48 valves.

| | |
|---|---|
| Displacement | 6.0 liter |
| Horsepower | 600 @ 6,000 rpm |
| Torque | 553 lb-ft @ 5,600 rpm |

**Drivetrain**
6-speed ZF automatic that can be operated in automatic mode or manual control via shift lever or shift paddle; continuous all-wheel drive.

**Suspension, handling, & braking**
Front double-wishbone/rear trapezoidal multilink with self-leveling air springs and continuous damping control; optional front and rear ventilated carbon-ceramic brakes with eight-piston calipers; adaptive cruise control system; antilock-brake and stability system with traction control.

**Weights and measurements**
| | |
|---|---|
| Curb weight | 5,478 lbs |
| Wheelbase | 108.1 in |
| Length | 189.1 in |
| Width | 86.4 in |
| Height | 55.0 in |
| Track F/R | 63.9/63.3 in |

**Performance**
| | |
|---|---|
| 0–60 mph (mfr est.) | 4.5 sec |
| Top speed (mfr est.) | 200 mph |
| Lateral acceleration | 1.2g |

# BMW M3 Coupé—Double the power, double the speed

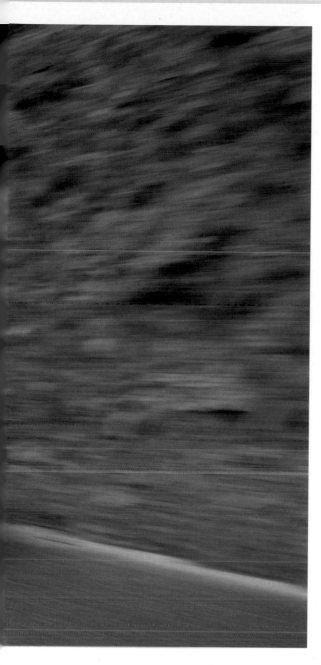

More than 20 years after the first M3 was met with rave reviews from the press and fear from its racetrack rivals, the German carmaker launched its fourth version in 2008—with both horsepower and cylinders doubled from the original. The latest generation is available in sedan, coupé, and folding-hardtop convertible forms. But don't be confused by the fact that you can order one with four doors. The M3's new V8 cranks out 414 horsepower, making it quicker than many classic two-seat sports cars. But it handles even better, and is a genuine rival even for sports car icons like the Porsche 911.

The "M" designation stands for motorsport, and BMW defines its M Series as sports cars with the amenities of a luxury car. 'The driver can cruise comfortably to get groceries in the city and afterwards he can go to the racetrack and improve his personal lap times,' explains Klaus Schmidt, the engineer in charge of chassis development. M cars have won a loyal, almost obsessive following; to create one, a standard BMW must be comprehensively re-engineered. Ordinary BMWs can be fitted with M bodykits and wheels, but don't be fooled; this is the real thing.

This M3 is the newest member of the M family. The M3 series was born with the second-generation 3 Series, known to aficionados as the E30, BMW's internal project designation. It was launched in 1986 with a 195 horsepower in-line four-cylinder engine, and was available in coupé or convertible form. It wasn't a powerhouse, but its sensational handling won it instant cult status. Its steering remains a benchmark for precision and feel. Subsequent M3s were created from the E36 and E46 3-Series, and featured gutsy inline six-cylinder engines. The current version—the first to feature a V8 engine—is referred to as the E90, E92 or E93 for the sedan, coupé and convertible.

The M3's price doesn't quite make it a sports car for the masses, but it has a substantially larger market than many sports cars, and the fact that BMW continues to raise the bar for both performance and refinement keeps it a target for competitors around the world, and an object of desire for drivers.

**Above:** Upgrades added to the car from the standard 3-Series models include more powerful and responsive engine, improvements in handling and suspension, more aggressive aerodynamics, and multiple interior and exterior accents.

**Left to right:** This model boasts M Double Spoke Satin Chrome finish light alloy wheels, an aluminum hood with powerdome, front and rear spoiler, flat-paneled underbody, and M exterior side-view mirrors with a double bridge in black.

# Vehicle Design

The M3 is M's take on the latest version of the BMW 3-Series, which made its debut in 2006. To a novice eye, the M3 looks more muscular but doesn't scream high performance; subtlety has always been an M hallmark. However, 80 percent of the vehicle is changed from the standard 3-Series, and car enthusiasts will quickly identify it by its flared front and rear fenders, lowered suspension, enlarged lower air intake, and the substantial bulge on the hood to accommodate the V8; BMW calls it the 'powerdome'. Other cues include vents in the fenders, exclusive wheels, quad exhausts, and, of course, the famous "M" badges.

The interior is simple, functional, and understated. Endlessly adjustable sport seats offer comfort and support whether racing around the track or cruising the autobahn. The M-design instrument cluster has titanium-ringed instrument dials with red needles, and the rev counter features a series of warning lights around its upper reaches that extinguish as the engine warms up, reminding the driver not to over-rev this aristocratic motor until it's ready. It's another reminder that you're not driving a standard, simple, idiot-proof 3-Series.

BMW is approaching a decade with its i-Drive information system, which is standard and displays on a well-shaded seven-inch screen. Though the M3 has an updated and simplified version that is more intuitive, it still requires the driver to use a rotary controller to navigate through a series of menus to operate systems such as the stereo and the satellite navigation, and many owners still have a love-hate relationship with it.

**Top:** The steering wheel is leather-wrapped with audio and phone controls, M color stitching and telescopic adjustment.

**Middle:** The interior is upholstered in anthracite with black cloth and leather upholstery.

**Bottom:** Interior features include an adjustable front armrest, door sills with the BMW M3 logo and folding rear-seat headrests.

# Performance

For years M-car fans waited for an eight-cylinder engine for the M3. They haven't been disappointed; the new V8 weighs only 30 pounds more than the inline six that it replaces, yet increases horsepower by nearly 20 percent. Wind the engine up to its stratospheric 8,300 rpm redline and its 414 horsepower propels the car to 60 miles per hour in a mere 4.4 seconds—cutting nearly a full second off the previous-generation M3. The car is available with a smooth six-speed manual transmission or hi-tech seven-speed dual-clutch unit adjustable for performance or comfort.

BMW has earned its reputation for creating the best-handling daily-driver cars in the world, and the M3 arguably performs better than any of its predecessors. Even with a 3,704-pound curb weight, the car carves the road as though hardwired to the driver's brain, yet can still cruise along with the comfort of a standard luxury siblings. That gentler side has some diehard fans wondering if the M badge has gone soft; some of the appeal of previous M3s was their raw and raucous demeanor. They might have a point, but this remains a sensational sports car, and anyone new to M-cars will simply be blown away by its amazing all-round ability.

## At a Glance

**Country of manufacture**
Germany

**Engine**
Front-mounted 4.0 liter V8 with Double VANOS steplessly variable valve timing, aluminum construction, dual overhead camshafts, and 4 valves per cylinder.

| | |
|---|---|
| Displacement | 4.0 liter |
| Horsepower | 414 @ 8,300 rpm |
| Torque | 295 lb-ft @ 3,900 rpm |

**Drivetrain**
6-speed manual transmission with additional oil cooler and heavy-duty dual-disc clutch; optional 7-speed M double-clutch transmission (M DCT) with Drivelogic with launch control.

**Suspension, handling, & braking**
Programmable suspension including four-wheel independent adjustable suspension; Servotronic steering assist, electronic dampers, antilock-brakes with cross-drilled and vented rotors, and stability system with traction control.

**Weights and measurements**

| | |
|---|---|
| Curb weight | 3,704 lbs |
| Wheelbase | 108.7 in |
| Length | 181.8 in |
| Height | 55.8 in |
| Fuel capacity | 20 gal |

**Performance**

| | |
|---|---|
| 0–60 mph | 4.4 sec |
| Top speed (mfr est.) | 155 mph |
| Redline | 8,300 rpm |
| Lateral acceleration | 0.95g |

# Bolwell Nagari—Fulfilling a boyhood dream

Extraordinary name, extraordinary car, extraordinary story. You might not have heard of the Bolwell Nagari, but once you've learned about it, you'll never forget it. How many carmakers emerge from a four-decade hibernation, resurrect their most successful model, and fufill the boyhood dream of their founders? Only Bolwell.

Campbell Bolwell loved cars as a kid, and built his first car with his brothers at the age of 16. Cobbled together from a 1938 Ford V8 chassis, it wasn't the prettiest car on the road, but it could outrun Austin Healeys and the other sports cars of the day. The young Australian launched his car company in 1962 at the age of 20, with his brothers Graeme and the late Winston. He studied racecar construction, went to welding classes, and soon released the lightweight Mk4 with a metal chassis and fiberglass body.

During the next few years his company built a handful of street and competition cars. In 1966, Graeme went to the United Kingdom. The Bolwells had always admired the technical prowess of Lotus's legendary founder Colin Chapman, so Graeme spent several months at Lotus assembling racecars.

By 1969, Bolwell had released the first Nagari, a front-engined sports car with a space frame chassis and fiberglass body powered by a Ford 302 cubic inch small-block V8. Eight hundred were sold before Bolwell steered his company away from carmaking and into the manufacture of advanced lightweight composite materials.

It has been a success, and now Bolwell has resurrected his passion to build a great sports car. The second version of the Bolwell Nagari was launched at the 2008 Melbourne Motor Show. Australians love their cars, and build some fine examples, but until now they haven't had a credible specialist sports car maker of the kind that flourishes elsewhere in the world, and especially in the United Kingdom. The reborn Bolwell may just provide that. If it's as good as it looks, Aussie buyers will flock to it, and the rest of the world might follow.

**Above:** The name of the car, Nagari, is an Aboriginal word that means "flowing". The Nagari was the first sports car manufactured by the company, with the latest model appearing at the 2008 Melbourne Motor Show powered by a supercharged 3.5 liter engine.

**Left to right:** The carbon-reinforced body and lightweight sub-frames developed for the engine, drivetrain, and suspension connected to a full carbon-fiber tub make the car similar to some of the world's most admired sports cars.

# Vehicle Design

Initial impressions of the Bolwell Nagari reveal a modern sports car with retro design cues that hint at a vintage Lotus or Lamborghini. Its nose is wide and simple with an air intake in the center feeding radiators that are vented out the top, and with brake ducts in the lower corners. The rear view of the car is dominated by the "flying buttress" C-pillars that extend from the roofline to the back of the quarter panels, and pay homage to the look of the original Nagari.

Its construction is similar to some supercars, with a full carbon-fiber tub connected to lightweight sub-frames for the engine, drivetrain, and suspension, and a carbon-reinforced body. This formula makes it extremely lightweight.

Though neither exotic nor opulent, the interior of the Nagari is complete and functional. Small manufacturers often rely on other companies for components, especially interiors. This gives the little guys the benefit of quality research and development, especially for highly complex interior assemblies. Including these creature comforts makes the car more user-friendly, and expands its potential market. Comfort and practicality are certainly important, but the Recaro racing seats with the Bolwell logo announce this car's true priorities.

**Top:** The Nagari is specifically designed to be able to deliver top performance on the punishing conditions of Australian roads.

**Middle:** The car features a six-speed paddle-shift transmission and is made of high-impact composites and carbon-fiber reinforcements that were originally developed for aviation and space programs.

**Bottom:** The front design of the Nagari is clean and simple, with air intake feeding radiators vented out of the top.

# Performance

Campbell Bolwell emphasizes that the fundamentals of performance engineering haven't changed since he was designing his first cars 50 years ago; only the materials he now works with have changed or improved. For the moment, the Nagari has a mid-mounted V6 borrowed from the Toyota Aurion that pumps out 295 horsepower and 254 pound-feet of torque. That is likely to change, as the Aurion is only available with an automatic transmission, and the Nagari production car is expected to have a six-speed sequential manual transmission with steering-wheel mounted paddle shifters.

A manual transmission and supercharger package are options for the Australian-built car. Performance is said to be potent, with a zero-to-60 time of four seconds or less, combined with the precise handling you'd expect given its light weight, stiff chassis, and the agile nature of mid-engined V6 sports cars. There is no word on an alternate engine or a left-hand-drive version, but its lineage and engineering earn it serious credibility from sports car fans, and its creation fulfils a 50-year dream for Campbell Bolwell himself.

## Breckland Beira—The best technologies, chosen by the experts

It's a classic formula for transforming British sports cars: take a small, lightweight open-top roadster and drop in a powerful American V8 to create a thrilling and often affordable new sports car with performance that dwarfs its size. But this time British sports car specialist Breckland Technology is dropping a big American engine into an American car.

Like Lotus, Breckland is a supplier to other car companies, providing manufacturing for limited-run or concept vehicles for clients such as Mosler. But, unlike Lotus, it hasn't put its name on a car until now. Created by combining the General Motors Kappa platform, which underpins the Pontiac Solstice and Saturn Sky, with the C5 Corvette's LS2 V8 engine, the Beira is the first car badged as a Breckland. Engineering director Mark Easton explains that Breckland 'didn't set out to reinvent the wheel with the Beira. The Kappa platform offers a highly competent chassis, which has been subjected to intensive crash and safety tests and is readily available.'

While the Beira is based on GM's rigid, hydro-formed chassis, nearly the whole car has been re-bodied, although the standard doors are retained for side-impact protection. It is made by hand from composite materials in the Breckland factory. By using so many GM parts, the company was able to minimize the research and development costs that sink so many sports car start-ups. It will also cut development time to less than a year, and produce a car that gives buyers 'maximum performance for money spent, and real individuality,' according to Breckland's Mike Rawlings. 'We wanted to showcase Breckland's design and engineering capabilities, and produce an exciting driver's car, with excellent handling dynamics, terrific performance, and great looks.'

Breckland has even managed to give the thunderous V8 a green makeover; it will now run on either gasoline or liquefied petroleum gas (LPG), stored in an 18-gallon onboard tank, giving the Beira a range of more than 700 miles. The longer you can enjoy that V8's performance for, the better.

**Above:** The Breckland Beira combines the GM Kappa platform also seen in the Pontiac Solstice and Opel GT with GM's 6-liter V8 engine. This is the first car to be branded under the Breckland name, the company having honed its experience building specialist cars for clients including Mosler.

**Left to right:** The engine has been fine-tuned to produce 397 horsepower and is joined by a Tremec six-speed gearbox—top speed is limited electronically to 155 mph but the car is capable of accelerating to 60 mph in less than 4.9 seconds.

# Vehicle Design

In reshaping GM's roadster, Breckland gave it a more muscular look, including a stronger nose, sleeker sides, and a stylish, fastback rear end with an integrated diffuser. It retains some family resemblance to the Saturn Sky, but draws design inspiration from classic British sports cars of the 1960s at the same time.

Targeted at budget-conscious sports car buyers, the GM interior lacks some of the individuality of other sports cars. While the fundamentals of the interior are retained, Breckland has upgraded it, with the most significant improvement being the greater use of leather and Alcantara—diamond-stitched on the seats, like a Bentley—as well as custom dash and console components that include an infotainment system from Clarion.

The seven-inch touch-screen plays DVDs, has iPod and Bluetooth connectivity, and 30-gigabyte navigation hard drive. An optional reversing camera can be displayed on the screen.

A significant benefit of adapting a GM platform is that this tiny firm can include systems that have been developed and tested to the standards of a major global player, but are hard to get right, such as air conditioning and airbags. Some buyers may lament the lack of a power hood, but these are are costly to engineer and can have a major impact on weight, trunk space, and exterior design.

**Top:** The 18-inch cast-alloy wheels are shod with ultra low-profile tires by Bridgestone. The buyer is also able to opt for 19-inch rims and rubber.

**Middle:** Headlights and rear quarter panels are the only throwbacks to the Opel GT donor car, with the rest of the bodywork being unique to the Beira.

**Bottom:** The cockpit is fitted with hand-stitched leather, Alcantara seats and trim, a Clarion multimedia system, power windows, and air conditioning.

# Performance

The Breckland Beira is almost completely reengineered by comparison with a standard Solstice, with major suspension, body, and interior enhancements. The pushrod V8 is constructed of aluminum and cranks out 397 horsepower, or more than double the output of the stock engine. Even with the bigger engine and additional LPG gas tank, the car weighs just over 3,000 pounds.

Suspension enhancements were engineered in partnership with KW Suspension, and include different springs, shock absorbers, and anti-roll bars. Powerful brakes from HiSpec have six pistons in the front and four pistons in the rear. The manufacturer's claimed 0-60 mph times may be significantly understated at "under five seconds", as Ferraris and Corvettes with similar power-to-weight ratios are in the low four-second range. But it's always better for a new sports car maker to under-promise and over-deliver. That's what made those big-engined Brit roadsters of the 1960s such a riot to drive, and sports car fans will be hoping the Beira will be the same.

## At a Glance

**Country of manufacture**
United Kingdom

**Engine**
Front-mounted, 6.0 liter General Motors LS2 'small block' pushrod V8 modified to run on both gasoline and LPG.

| | |
|---|---|
| Displacement | 6.0-liter |
| Horsepower | 397 @ 6,000 rpm |
| Torque | 400 lb-ft @ 4,400 rpm |
| Rev limit | 7,000 rpm |

**Drivetrain**
Tremec close-ratio 6-speed manual transmission sending power to the rear wheels through a limited-slip differential.

**Suspension, handling, & braking**
Fully Independent suspension with KW monotube shock absorbers and springs; front and rear vented and slotted disc brakes with 6-piston calipers in front and 4-piston calipers in rear.

**Weights and measurements**

| | |
|---|---|
| Curb weight | 3,086 lbs |
| Wheelbase | 95.1 in |
| Length | 165.2 in |
| Width | 76.5 in |
| Height | 50.1 in |

**Performance**

| | |
|---|---|
| 0–60 mph (mfr est) | <4.9 sec |
| Top speed (governed) | 155 mph |

**Trivia**
Biera is a city in Mozambique, an ancient province of Portugal, and loosely translated from Portuguese means "on the brink of."

# Bugatti Veyron 16.4 Grand Sport—The fastest coupé becomes the fastest convertible

There may never be another car like the Bugatti Veyron. At its launch, it was quite simply the fastest, most powerful, most expensive car ever put into series production. Some experts believe it replaces the venerable McLaren F1 as the greatest sports car ever produced; others believe that the simpler, lighter, and better-handling F1 is still the better car. But it will be almost impossible to better the Veyron's incredible statistics without seriously compromising safety, reliability, refinement, and usability. You might go faster by strapping four wheels to a rocket, but the Veyron is also sybaritic in its luxury and surprisingly simple to drive. Now the Grand Sport version claims the title of the world's fastest convertible, and gives the Veyron's fabulously wealthy customers the excuse to buy another one.

Ettore Bugatti—hence the EB logo—was born into an artistic family in Italy and founded his automotive company in France. During the 1920s and 30s, his cars won countless prestigious races, and examples of his engineering and artistic masterpieces sell for millions at auction. The company faded after World War II. The first serious revival attempt culminated with production of the superb EB110, but was killed by the recession of the early '90s. Volkswagen purchased the rights to the name in 1998 and began working on the world's fastest car.

The Veyron is one of a few cars that lay claim to the title of fastest production car in the world, with a top speed of more than 253 miles per hour. But Bugatti has sold nearly 300 Veyrons, while its rivals' volumes pale in comparison. And all three claimants have broken the 250 mph barrier with distinctly different tracks and conditions so, without a head-to-head test, it's impossible to say which is faster. And slightly irrelevant too; how many roads in the world are long and straight and smooth enough to let you travel at a third of the speed of sound?

**Above:** The Bugatti Veyron EB 16.4 was introduced in 2005 as the fastest production car in the world. It remains one of the fastest accelerating and decelerating production cars, reaching 100 mph in just 8.6 seconds.

**Left to right:** The car is named after French racing driver Pierre Veyron, who won Le Mans in 1939 for the original Bugatti company. The car is handcrafted in a factory near the former Bugatti headquarters in Château St Jean in Molsheim, France.

# Vehicle Design

Under then-chairman Ferdinand Piëch, Volkswagen commissioned Giorgetto Guigiaro, of ItalDesign, to produce several Bugatti concept cars, including an 18-cylinder version. The production version, christened the Veyron 16.4 and its lofty performance goals of 1001hp and 400 kilometres per hour, caused some cynicism.

The models are named for the winner of the 24 Hours of Le Mans, Pierre Veyron, with the "16" and "4" indicating the number of cylinders and turbochargers respectively. The Bugatti's spec sheet reads like a fantasy car, with its plasma-coated cylinder liners, titanium pistons, and magnesium valve caps.

Delivery of the 300 production coupés was scheduled to begin in 2003, but was delayed as engineers struggled with both heating and high-speed handling issues. Production finally began in 2005.

The Grand Sport made its world premiere in August 2008 in Pebble Beach, and features a removable roof made of lightweight, transparent polycarbonate, and a weather-resistant interior. One hundred and fifty cars were announced for the production run, with the first 40 reserved for current coupé owners.

**Top:** A unique alloy was developed to ensure the most consistent possible aluminum shine to complement the choicest leather, selected only if free from blemishes.

**Middle:** The light-alloy steering wheel is composed of aluminum spokes, leather cover, and rocker switches to improve access to the sports automatics functions.

**Bottom:** The Veyron was the first car to include adapted Burmester sound system elements originally developed for home use.

# Performance

Any cynicism was misplaced. By the end of the 2005, the Veyron had cracked the production car speed record, twice. A Koenigsegg had recently hit 241 mph to break the McLaren F1's decade-old record, but Bugatti broke it again with runs of 248.5 and then 252.95 mph. Its unique W16 configuration (four banks of four mated together) was engineered to be compact enough to fit into the space of a typical 12-cylinder engine. All the horsepower is transmitted to a seven-speed dual-clutch computer-controlled manual transmission that drivers can command with paddle shifters or operate in "automatic" mode. All-wheel drive splits the power among four run-flat Michelin tires that together cost as much as a MINI Cooper. This configuration means it can hit 62 miles per hour in 2.5 seconds—easily as fast as a modern Formula 1 car—but all the driver has to do is select the right transmission mode, and hold the throttle to the floor. What happens next threatens to overwhelm the central nervous system; the absurd, terrifying thrust only starts to let up once you're way beyond 200mph. There is simply nothing else like it on the road, and there may never be a car to eclipse it.

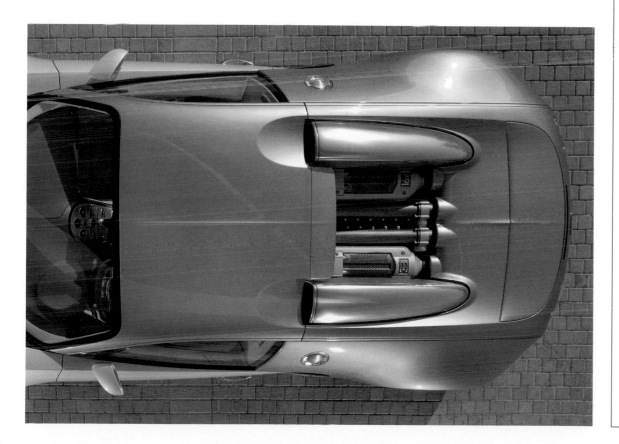

## At a Glance

**Country of manufacture**
France

**Engine**
Rear-mid mounted aluminum narrow-angle 16-cylinder in "W" configuration with quad superchargers, direct injection, 64 valves.

| | |
|---|---|
| Displacement | 8.0 liter |
| Horsepower | 1,001 @ 6,000 rpm |
| Torque | 923 lb-ft @ 2,200-5,500 rpm |
| Rev limit | 6,600 rpm |

**Drivetrain**
Ricardo 7-speed electronic dual-clutch gearbox, all-wheel-drive system.

**Suspension, handling, & braking**
Fully independent multi-link suspension, vented carbon-ceramic brakes.

**Weights and measurements**

| | |
|---|---|
| Curb weight | 4,387 lbs |
| Wheelbase | 106.7 in |
| Length | 175.7 in |
| Width | 78.7 in |
| Height | 47.4 in |

**Performance**

| | |
|---|---|
| 0–62 mph (mfr est.) | 2.5 sec |
| Quarter mile | 9.8 sec |
| Top speed | 253 mph |

**Trivia**

When the coupé debuted at Pebble Beach, the light blue/silver paint scheme had mistakenly been applied with the colors inverted—all the silver areas should have been light blue, and vice versa.

# Chevrolet Corvette ZR1—The $100,000 "Blue Devil" project

Rick Wagoner's casual comment is sure to become an automotive urban legend. Talking about the Corvette Z06 chassis, the former General Motors CEO asked, 'Geez, if that's what you can do with $60,000, I wonder what a $100,000 Corvette would look like?'

With those words, the Corvette team went to work exploring the upper reaches of sports car performance, according to Corvette Engineer Tadge Juechter, in a *Motor Trend* interview. The project's internal codename was "Blue Devil", the team name of Wagoner's alma mater, Duke University, and speculation on the project mounted each year as evidence of a "Super Corvette" leaked to an eager press.

Six years after his first remark, Wagoner got his answer. It's one that the traditional supercar makers were none too happy about; at its launch in late 2008, the Corvette ZR1 bested cars on the track that cost two to three times as much. GM hadn't just developed a car people thought was good value for the extra price, or even the best Corvette in its storied half-century history. It has made, by common consent, one of the best performance cars ever.

The Corvette started out in 1953 as a weak attempt at an American version of popular European sports cars. It was fitted with a six-cylinder converted truck engine and two-speed automatic transmission, and had generally forgettable handling and braking. The advent of the Chevrolet-General Motors small block engine, combined with the inspiration of engineer Zora Arkus-Duntov to drop it into the 'Vette with a three-speed manual transmission, breathed life into a brand that is now synonymous with performance. Until the new ZR1 arrived, the highest performance version of the C5 and C6 'Vettes was the Z06, named for the option package on the order sheet. Based on the C6 sixth-generation Corvette platform, the ZR1 resurrects the name used on top-of-the-line models of the 1970s and 1990s, but completely eclipses them.

**Above:** The chassis of the ZR1 is made of aluminum and, to cut weight, many of the panels are of carbon-fiber, including the fenders, hood, roof, splitter, and rocker extensions, all protected with a special paint treatment to prevent sun damage.

**Left to right:** The ZR1 is the most powerful production Corvette to date, with a modified LS9 engine. This has a sixth-generation Eaton TVS R2300 roots-style four-lobe supercharger with an intercooler to improve efficiency. The supercharger's output was split into halves to avoid changes to the hood appearance.

# Vehicle Design

Though instantly recognizable as a Corvette, changes to the ZR1 are easily noticed. Firstly, the intercooler atop the engine is visible through a clear polycarbonate window in the hood, which has a conspicuous bulge to accommodate the supercharged engine.

Though the wider, lower, more athletic stance indicates that the car is something special, many of the body enhancements that help make the car a world-beater aren't readily apparent. To offset the additional weight of the supercharger, engineers used a substantial number of carbon-fiber components, including the fenders, rocker moldings, and a front splitter that is three times deeper than on the Z06. Some bare carbon-fiber parts are visible to onlookers, including the roof, roof bow, and underside of the hood.

Continuing a typical General Motors weakness, the interior falls short of supercar expectations, but does have notable upgrades from regular versions. ZR1 enhancements include logos embroidered on the headrests and emblazoned on the sill plates and tachometer, the addition of a boost gauge, and, most significantly, a special gauge cluster with a 220-mile-per-hour speedometer. An optional "luxury" package includes special seats, a custom leather interior, a navigation system, Bluetooth connectivity, and more.

**Top:** Functional fender vents provide engine cooling.

**Middle:** The use of carbon fiber is extensive throughout the ZR1. The wider fenders are made of carbon fiber, as are the hood, roof panel, roof bow, front fascia splitter and rocker moldings.

**Bottom:** The front brake rotors are the same design, in carbon-ceramic, as used in the Ferrari FXX track car with a reduction in diameter to 15.5 inches for extra wheel clearance.

# Performance

Twenty-five years ago, a 6.9-second zero-to-60 time put a car atop the performance charts. The ZR1 can hit 60mph in just 3.3 seconds; give it 6.9 seconds and it will hit 100 mph. A quarter-mile time of just over 11 seconds at 130 miles per hour and a 205 mph top speed earn it supercar credentials.

This performance comes courtesy of a 638 horsepower, 6.2-liter LS9 pushrod V8, equipped with a supercharger. As in the Z06, hi-tech engine components include titanium connecting rods and exhaust valves, and a dry-sump oiling system. Everything in the rear transaxle gearbox has been strengthened to handle the massive power.

The ZR1's Active Handling System incorporates magnetorheological shock absorbers and race-bred double-wishbone suspension design to help the car achieve more than 1g of lateral grip and cope with the massive speed and forces generated by that engine. Makes you wonder what they could do with $200,000…

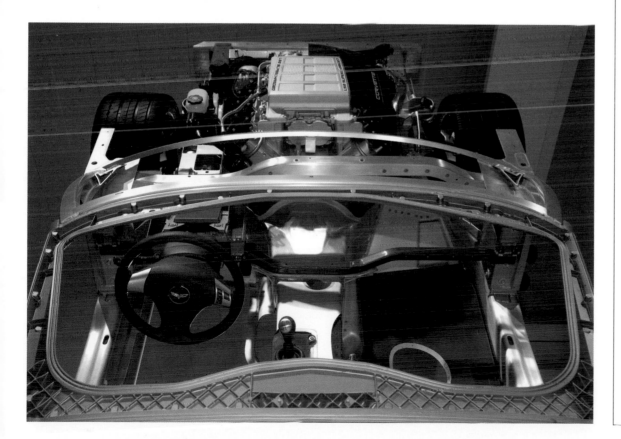

## At a Glance

**Country of manufacture**
United States

**Engine**
Front-mounted, LS9 SOHC pushrod engine with aluminum block and heads, 2 valves per cylinder, and Eaton supercharger with 4-lobe Roots-style blower.

| | |
|---|---|
| Displacement | 6.2 liter |
| Horsepower | 638 @ 6,500 rpm |
| Torque | 604 lb-ft @ 3,800 rpm |
| Maximum boost | 10.5 psi |
| Rev limit | 6,500 rpm |

**Drivetrain**
Rear-mounted close-ratio 6-speed manual transaxle with dual-disc clutch.

**Suspension, handling, & braking**
Front and rear short/long arm (SLA) double-wishbone suspension with forged-aluminum A-arms and transverse composite springs, magnetorheological shock absorbers with "tour" and "sport" mode, cross-drilled Brembo carbon-ceramic brakes with 6-piston front calipers and 4-piston rear.

**Weights and measurements**

| | |
|---|---|
| Curb weight | 3,350 lbs |
| Wheelbase | 105.7 in |
| Length | 176.2 in |
| Weight distribution | 52/48 |

**Performance**

| | |
|---|---|
| 0–60 mph | 3.3 sec |
| 0–100 mph | 6.9 sec |
| Quarter mile (est.) | 11.2 @ 130.5 mph |
| Top speed | 205 mph |

# Dodge Viper SRT10—Adding extra venom to the icon

In the late eighties, Chrysler's "car guy" top executives—Lee Iacocca and Bob Lutz —decided that their company, and indeed the nation, needed a high-performance halo car in the spirit of the original Shelby Cobra.

America was stuck in the horsepower doldrums. Zero-to-60 mile-per-hour times under ten seconds were a rarity among American cars, and even high-priced European supercars of the era struggled to break under five seconds. So when the car they conceived—the Viper RT/10 Roadster—started rolling off the assembly line in early 1992, it felt like it had arrived from another planet. It had an eight-liter V10 engine; staggering even now. While its 400 horsepower was impressive, its 465 pound-feet of torque was downright eye-popping, and good for a 4.6-second zero-to-60 time; faster than virtually all but Ferrari's extreme F40.

The car went from design concept to production in slightly more than three years—a near impossibility in the sluggish American car industry of the time—and the legendary Carroll Shelby himself was instrumental in the car's development. True to the spirit of its Cobra inspiration, the Viper was a pure, raw sports car. Those first cars had a soft removable roof and, as the nameplate matured, a coupé was introduced that featured "double-bubble" fixed-head styling, to allow room for helmets.

The car earned a following in Europe and commanded respect on racetracks on both sides of the Atlantic Ocean as Team Oreca, from France, campaigned the cars extensively. The factory-supported program reached its zenith with three consecutive class wins and an overall win in the 2000 Rolex 24 Hours of Daytona. Privateer teams still race current-generation cars in various sports car series.

Now in its fourth generation, the Viper has its position etched in sports car history. With outrageous looks and performance, it's the only car to have cheered up an entire nation.

**Above:** The Viper's performance hood is built with larger air extractors and louver screens as well as an enlarged center scoop to give true ram-air capability.

**Left to right:** The design of the car includes styling cues such as swept-back fenders and deep-cut side scallops. The car comes with two choices of body style and a selection of exterior colors. The electrical system has been improved to include a 180-amp alternator, twin electric cooling fans, electronic throttles, and a new VENOM engine-management system.

# Vehicle Design

The original roadster was a targa with a removable top that resembled a toupé when in place, and detachable side flaps with plastic windows. There was a conspicuous absence of creature comforts. The most notable omission was air conditioning, especially with blistering engine heat permeating the floor. And while the side exhausts looked cool, many a romantic date ended with a cold compress pressed onto burned legs.

Each generation of the Viper has undergone evolutionary styling and technology improvements rather than complete makeovers, and the newest SRT—for Street and Racing Technology—is no different. Though it appears wider than the original, it's merely that the creases are sharper and the Dodge crossbar grille more pronounced. But, if anything, the look has become even more intimidating, with the addition of nearly as many hood vents as a shark has gills.

The current model is available in coupé form or as a full convertible. Though the interior will never be mistaken for that of a luxury car, it now has the creature comforts buyers expect for a night on the town, or even a weekend away. Leather-trimmed race seats with massive side-bolsters, air conditioning, and a logical gauge cluster lie within. Even an upgraded sound system and satellite navigation system are offered, but it's the provocative styling and prodigious power—and not the gadgets—that move these cars off the sales floor.

**Top:** The race-inspired cockpit includes bolstered, leather-trimmed front bucket seats with suede Microfiber inserts and accent stitching.

**Middle:** The cockpit has been designed with both control and comfort in mind.

**Bottom:** The dash is accented with satin chrome, with a 220 mph speedometer, easy-to-reach gear shifter and aluminum, power-adjustable pedals.

# Performance

With a round 600 horsepower pumping from the enlarged 8.4-liter V10, the Viper runs zero-to-60 times in the mid-three-second range, has a 202 mph top speed, and so is clearly both sports car and supercar. Setting the quickest time around the infamous, tortuous Nürburgring race circuit in Germany is the ultimate achievement for some sports car afficionados, and the record was set in August 2008 by a Viper ACR (American Club Racer), a track-day version of the car.

Structural integrity and suspension enhancements have improved handling through the years, with probably the biggest improvement being made to the brakes. For years, the car lost head-to-head comparisons to slower cars due to weak anchors, and the problem persisted when even antilock was added.

Bigger rotors gripped by stronger Brembo calipers have shortened 60-to-zero brake distances to less than 100 feet. Couple that with lateral grip of more than 1g, and the Viper now stops and steers as well as it goes. And it goes very hard indeed.

## At a Glance

**Country of manufacture**
United States

**Engine**
Mid-front-mounted, 90-degree V10 with aluminum block, variable valve timing, race-inspired oiling system.

| | |
|---|---|
| Displacement | 8.4 liter |
| Horsepower | 600 @ 6,000 rpm |
| Torque | 560 lb-ft @ 5,100 rpm |
| Rev limit | 6,250 rpm |

**Drivetrain**
Tremec 6-speed manual transmission with low-inertia twin-disc clutch, limited-slip rear differential.

**Suspension, handling, & braking**
Fully independent upper and lower A-arm suspension with high-performance aluminum control arms and knuckles, lightweight coil-over shock absorbers; front and rear vented and slotted Brembo disk brakes with 6-piston calipers in front and 4-piston calipers in rear.

**Weights and measurements**

| | |
|---|---|
| Curb weight | 3,440 lbs |
| Wheelbase | 98.8 in |
| Length | 175.7 in |
| Track F/R | 57.8/60.9 in |

**Performance**

| | |
|---|---|
| 0–60 mph | 3.4 sec |
| 0–100 mph | 8.2 |
| Quarter mile | 11.7 @ 122.8 mph |
| Lateral grip | 1.13g |
| Top speed | 202 mph (governed) |

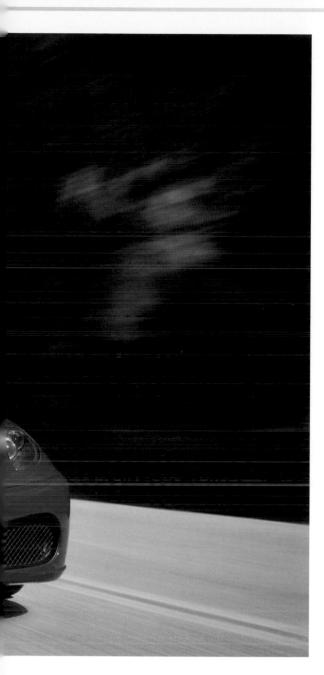

# Ferrari F430 Scuderia Spider 16M—Formula 1 on the city streets

Just by its name, the Ferrari Scuderia Spider 16M illustrates the rich history of the famous badge it bears. One hundred years after founder Enzo Ferrari attended his first race as a boy, the legendary Italian carmaker announced its latest masterpiece. "Scuderia" is the name of Ferrari's race team. "16M" represents the number of Formula 1 constructor championships the marque has won in over 60 years of competition, and the "Spider" convertible body style has been a mainstay of the company's vehicle line since its earliest models. Put them together and you get the car built to celebrate Ferrari's victory in the 2008 Formula 1 Constructor's World Championship.

Enzo spent nearly 20 years associated with Alfa Romeo as a racecar builder and driver, up until the eve of World War II. He started Ferrari in its current form in 1947. Since attending that race at 10 years old, his true passion was racing, and the automobile world is fortunate he had to build street cars to fund his teams.

The F430 traces its roots to the 1960s, when Ferrari manufactured less expensive V6 and V8 vehicles under the Dino brand. Ferrari branding on its venerable V8 series started in the 1970s with the mid-engined 308, and subsequent coupé and convertible models brought more power, reliability, and technology to the market, in the 328, 348, 355, and 360 models.

Arguably one of the greatest sports cars of all time, the F430 was launched in 2004, and its racing heritage is apparent in virtually every aspect of its design. Ferrari created a single-brand "Challenge" racing series in 1993 with track versions of the 348 Berlinetta, and continued it with subsequent models. The 430 Scuderia follows the 360 Stradale as a stripped-down, street-legal version of the Challenge racing car that gives up some comfort for improved power and handling, and produces a car that somehow manages to be even more exciting than the standard model.

**Above:** The latest addition to the new generation of V8-engined sportsc ars from Ferrari, the Spider includes all the F430's technology and was developed through close collaboration with the Formula 1 racing division.

**Left to right:** The Scuderia's experience has influenced the car, from the innovations in aerodynamics, which have been honed to generate special flows that improve cooling and increase the downforce, to the F1 transmission with upgraded software and compact, automatic electric hood.

# Vehicle Design

The visual changes to the Scuderia models over the standard F430 are substantial. The shark-nose front is accentuated by bolder air intakes, a more pronounced splitter, and redesigned center inlet. Add in the Formula 1-style venturi diffuser at the rear of the car and lower suspension, and the resulting differences in airflow help keep the car pressed to the road at high speeds without the wings and other aerodynamic addenda that increase drag.

The interior of the Scuderia is about the business of racing. Everything other than climate control is there to help the driver get around a track safely and quickly. Glove-soft leather hides have been replaced with carbon-fiber and Alcantara. There is a fire extinguisher strapped to the passenger floor, racing buckets in place of the typical Daytona-style seat, and the optional chunky carbon-fiber steering wheel has LEDs that light up in sequence as the engine approaches its screaming 8,640 rpm redline.

Among the changes to the Spider 16M are a removable Ferrari iPod Touch with a central dock, and a carbon-fiber outer shell on the roll bars. Only 499 Spider 16Ms will be built.

**Top:** The engine is visible at all times through the fully automatic electric hood, which has its own automatic body-colored tonneau cover.

**Middle:** The cockpit has been increased in size, with a slimmer central tunnel to house the gear lever turret, on the manual version, or F1 console, on the paddle-shift.

**Bottom:** New inserts on the dash can be personalized in carbon or aluminum. The same materials have been extended to the front of the tunnel.

# Performance

The Scuderia coupé established its credentials when, with Formula 1 star Michael Schumacher at the wheel, it ran a lap of Ferrari's Fiorano test track quicker than Ferrari's 2003, V12-powered Enzo hypercar; that's how quickly Ferrari sports cars develop. Its 3.1-second zero-to-60 time also beat the Enzo's, and by four-tenths of a second. While the Spider is heavier than the coupé, performance numbers will likely be similar, as it is still 176 pounds lighter than a stock F430 Spider.

A vast array of Formula 1-inspired mechanical goodies engineered for the coupé carry over to the Spider. Among them, the steering wheel-mounted manettino selector with five settings that adjust transmission shifts and suspension response, as well as reaction from the antilock brakes, traction, and stability systems.

Driving the Scuderia is a more visceral experience than the regular F430; there's more noise and less comfort in the track-oriented car. But for buyers looking for the ultimate top-down driving experience, there are few sports cars as intoxicating as this very special Ferrari.

## At a Glance

**Country of manufacture**
Italy

**Engine**
Rear-mid-mounted 90-degree V8

| | |
|---|---|
| Displacement | 4.3 liter |
| Horsepower | 510 @ 8,500 rpm |
| Torque | 347 lb-ft @ 5,250 rpm |
| Rev limit | 8,640 rpm |

**Drivetrain**
6-speed F1 with paddle shifters, dry dual, electronic differential E-diff.

**Suspension, handling, & braking**
Independent double-wishbone adjustable suspension with titanium helical springs, lightweight electronic shock absorbers; stability and traction control systems controlled by steering wheel manettino; antilock brake system with 6-piston front and rear calipers, and carbo-ceramic disc.

**Weights and measurements**

| | |
|---|---|
| Curb weight | 3,175 lbs |
| Wheelbase | 107.1 in |
| Length | 177.6 in |
| Height | 47.9 in |
| Track F/R | 65.7/63.2 in |
| Weight distribution | 43/57 |

**Performance**

| | |
|---|---|
| 0–62 mph (mfr est) | 3.7 sec |
| Top speed (mfr est) | 195 mph |

**Trivia**
The F430 coupé had a cameo appearance in the 2006 Walt Disney blockbuster, *Cars*, voiced by Michael Schumacher.

# Ford Mustang Shelby GT500—The pony car with impressive performance

As it nears its first half-century, the Mustang isn't just one of the most enduring nameplates in the sports car world, but in the entire automotive firmament. During the five generations since its introduction in 1964, it has soldiered on through recessions, emissions, and disco. It has outlasted all of its direct competitors, though some have been revived, and continues to attract drivers of all ages and budgets.

Road and racecar legend Carroll Shelby was a renowned tuner in the early years, and rekindled his relationship with the car after the current model was launched in 2005. The Mustang even gave birth to—and indirectly gave its name to—its own class of sports car. The "pony car" is an affordable, compact, stylish American coupé with a performance image; the Mustang is its poster boy.

The 'Stang was launched to fill Ford's sports car gap when the Thunderbird grew into a luxury car. Then, as now, it was available with a choice of six- or eight-cylinder engines and manual or automatic transmissions. Subsequent generations of cars had larger and smaller bodies, and, at one point, an anaemic 88-horsepower four-cylinder embarrassment was offered as the base engine. Yet the Mustang had staying power, due in no small measure to its loyal fans.

After a full 25 years on the same Fox platform, the latest generation shares underpinnings with other rear-drive Ford products, including the Thunderbird, Jaguar S-Type, and Lincoln LS. Fans welcomed the retro styling, but were disappointed that the antiquated live rear axle stayed.

This GT500 model is the latest in a dizzying array of special editions on the current version, and it carries the Ford sports car heritage forward with aplomb.

**Above:** The 540 horsepower, 5.4-liter, 32-valve supercharged and intercooled engine has Tremac six-speed manual transmission and complements the SVT performance-tuned suspension components.

**Left to right:** The 19-inch wheels are forged aluminum, with P255/40ZR19 front and rear performance tires. The car's styling is unique, from the front and rear facia treatments to the unique hood with functional air extractors and the racing stripe and GT500 bodyside stripe.

# Vehicle Design

The fifth-generation Mustang draws much of its design inspiration from the 1967-68 models. It incorporates classic Mustang cues, including C-scoops in the sides, three-element tail lamps, and of course, the iconic galloping horse on the grille.

'We weren't just redesigning a car; we were adding another chapter to an epic,' says J Mays, Ford's Chief Creative Officer. The car was updated for the 2010 model year, and the GT500 builds on that new look.

'We worked with Carroll on this car very closely and everything we did on this was approved by him and I think this is the most powerful, coolest Mustang ever done,' said Ford Chief Designer, Doug Gaffka.

Available in coupé or convertible form, it's plainly a muscle car, with a front chin splitter, hood air extractor, and rear wing. Stripes are available in red, white, or silver, and are replicated on the seats. Interior enhancements include Alcantara material on the seats and steering wheel, as well as aluminum panels with what Ford describes as a 'three-dimensional dimpled texture pattern inspired by racing clutch plates, braided hoses, and cross-drilled racing brake rotors.'

**Top:** The sports bucket seats have leather surfaces with stripe-stitching to color coordinate with the vehicle's exterior.

**Middle:** Safety features on the car include side-impact airbags and dual front airbags, as well as a tire-pressure-monitoring system.

**Bottom:** The six-gauge instrument cluster includes SVT graphics and a reversed tachometer and speedometer.

# Performance

Performance variants haven't just been the domain of Shelby. Renowned tuners and racecar builders Roush, Steeda, and Saleen have all produced hot Mustangs with full factory blessing. Ford itself has offered nearly a dozen performance or design editions, most notably Cobras, SVT Cobras, SVOs, and Bullitts.

The GT500 moniker first appeared 1967 in a big-block V8 car with horsepower in the mid-300 range. For 2010, it starts out with a supercharged and intercooled 5.4-liter dual overhead cam engine that produces 540 horsepower and 510 pound-feet of torque.

Power from the front-mounted engine is transmitted to the rear wheels via a six-speed manual Tremec gearbox with a twin-disc clutch and a solid rear axle with Panhard rod. Those supercar-standard power and torque figures mean the GT500 will hit 60mph in just 4.1 seconds—if you can handle the wheelspin—and its top speed has to be restricted to 155 mph. This is a muscle car that can run with the supercars.

## At a Glance

**Country of manufacture**
United States

**Engine**
Front-mounted, supercharged 5.4-liter DOHC engine; cold air induction system.

| | |
|---|---|
| Displacement | 5.4 liter |
| Horsepower | 540 @ 6,200 rpm |
| Torque | 510 lb-ft @ 4,500 rpm |
| Rev limit | 6,250 rpm |

**Drivetrain**
Tremec close-ratio twin-disc 6-speed manual transmission sending power to the rear wheels.

**Suspension, handling, & braking**
Independent front suspension with Reverse-L independent MacPherson struts, stabilizer bar; three-link solid axle with coil springs, Panhard rod, stabilizer bar; antilock brakes with 4-piston Brembo calipers front and 2-piston rear, vented discs front and rear; traction control and stability system.

**Weights and measurements**

| | |
|---|---|
| Curb weight | 3,924 lbs |
| Wheelbase | 107.1 in |
| Length | 188.2 in |
| Width | 73.9 in |
| Height | 54.5 in |
| Track F/R | 61.9/63.0 in |
| Weight distribution | 58/42 |

**Performance**

| | |
|---|---|
| 0–60 mph (mfr est.) | 4.1 sec |
| Quarter mile (mfr est.) | 12.1 sec |
| Top speed | 155 mph (governed) |

# Gumpert Apollo—A car descended from the gods

If you're going to name your supercar after a Greek god, it had better be good. The German-made Gumpert Apollo lives up to its billing. The car was conceived in 2001 with the intention of creating one of the world's great sports cars. Roland Gumpert was the driving force behind it and gave the new company its distinctive name. It might not match Lamborghini or Ferrari for aural appeal, but the Gumpert name comes with ready-made racing heritage. Under Roland's leadership, Audi Quattros won 25 rounds in the World Rally Championship and four WRC titles. Gumpert's connection to Audi is evident, as the Apollo's engine and many interior components are sourced from his former employer, notably the bombproof, twin-turbocharged V8 engine that generates between 650 and 800 horsepower.

Production of the menacing-looking Apollo began in 2005, and the company delivered its 40th vehicle exactly three years later. 'From the first ideas to the start of production was a long and difficult journey,' says Roland. But it's always that way for ambitious sports car start-ups trying to take on the big players with their deep pockets.

With its steel tube frame and carbon-fiber body, the Apollo is more racecar than road car, and meets the FIA racing safety rules, making it one of the best road cars to have an accident in. It's so nearly a racer that it took just three months to prepare one for the 2008 24 Hours of Nürburgring, and that includes equipping it with a revolutionary hybrid drive system. The car didn't win the race, but it did build the company's race pedigree and demonstrated the effectiveness of hybrid technology on the track, now adopted by Formula 1.

The company is building a worldwide dealer network, which it expects will help it double annual production. Distributors are in place in Europe, the Middle East, and the United States, where cars are sold as a "modular" product. The cars and engines are brought in separately and assembled in the United States as kit cars so they don't have to undergo federal testing. But, as you'll see, this is no home-build special.

**Above:** The design challenge taken up by the Apollo's designers was to develop a car that combined the aerodynamics of a pure sportscar with the aesthetics of an exclusive vehicle—the car's silhouette, for example, was optimized in a number of wind tunnel tests.

**Left to right:** The underbody is encased in carbon, combining with the front diffuser and flow channels to achieve a particularly high negative lift for the vehicle. The forward cockpit position combines with the long wheelbase to ensure optimum drive quality.

# Vehicle Design

Roland Gumpert believes the cars he and the company's 45 employees provide everything a sports car buyer needs, namely quality, exclusivity, and technology. He wants your reaction to be instinctive. 'The customer should stand in front of it and say, '"Wow, that's a great car. I want it".'

The Apollo easily qualifies for supercar status with its massive power, race-bred suspension, exotic construction, and spectacular design. Two design features that always draw a crowd at shows are the massive gull-wing doors and the air intake scoop on the roof. The Apollo's wheels are pushed to the extreme corners of the car and the three huge air intakes in front and menacing trapezoidal headlamps all but scowl at onlookers.

The interior is essentially everything you'd expect to see in a racecar, but presented in a well-organized format with some luxury touches. Constraining weight is paramount, but the vehicle still comes with air conditioning, navigation, and an integrated backup camera.

Apollos are only built to the buyer's specification, and buyers at this level are pretty choosy, so the company has some flexibility to customize it to their taste. Even built-in air jacks that shoot down from the body to lift the entire car for a tyre change at the racetrack are an option. Try using them at the service station and watch people's reaction.

**Top:** The seat position is adjusted to suit the individual driver, using padding, upholstery, adjustable pedals, and the steering column.

**Middle:** The instrument panel is made of carbon-fiber; other features of the cockpit include air conditioning, a high-end navigation system with reverse camera, and DVD player.

**Bottom:** The wheels of the Apollo are aluminum cast with center lock.

# Performance

The twin-turbocharged Audi engine powering the Apollo generates 650 horsepower and an even more impressive 627 pound-feet of torque at 4,000 rpm. With its curb weight of less than 2,500 pounds, the car can hit 62 miles per hour in three seconds. Its 224 mph top speed may not set any records, but it puts it near the top of the sports car pile.

But it's not just about straight-line speed. The combination of power, handling, and the phenomenal braking of its eight-piston calipers helped the Gumpert set the record for the fastest lap around the *Top Gear* television show test track in Surrey, England. It bested cars costing two and three times as much, including the mighty Bugatti Veyron.

'It has always been my dream to have a car with so much downforce, such aero-dynamic efficiency that you could drive on the roof of a tunnel at high speed,' said Gumpert. 'This car can do it.'

## At a Glance

**Country of manufacture**
Germany

**Engine**
Rear-mid Audi-sourced twin-turbocharged DOHC V8 with dry-sump lubrication, 5 valves per cylinder and VarioCam variable valve timing.

| | |
|---|---|
| Displacement | 4.2 liter |
| Horsepower | 650 @ 6,500 rpm |
| Torque | 627 lb-ft @ 4,000 rpm |
| Rev limit | 7,200 rpm |

**Drivetrain**
6-speed sequential manual transmission sending power to the rear wheels; CIMA 6-speed sequential manual gearbox with Sachs twin-plate clutch; Torsen locking differential.

**Suspension, handling, & braking**
Front and rear double-wishbone suspension with inboard adjustable shock absorbers; ventilated disc brakes with 8-piston calipers.

**Weights and measurements**

| | |
|---|---|
| Curb weight | 2,425 lbs |
| Wheelbase | 106.3 in |
| Length | 175.6 in |
| Width | 78.6 in |
| Height | 43.8 in |
| Track F/R | 65.7/62.9 in |
| Weight distribution | 42/58 |

**Performance**

| | |
|---|---|
| 0–62 mph (mfr est) | 3.0 sec |
| Top speed (mfr est) | 224 mph |

# Honda S2000CR–One rockin' roadster

With its four-cylinder engine, modest 237 hp output and equally modest pricetag, the Honda S2000 represents the very opposite end of the sports car scale to monsters like the Bugatti Veyron. But sports cars shouldn't be judged on their sticker price, and lightweight, low-powered roadsters often provide the most fun you can have on four wheels. This car exemplifies these truths.

Born the son of a blacksmith and a weaver, the story of the challenges Soichiro Honda faced in launching his company is a favorite among motivational speakers. As a boy, he was enthralled by engines and the machines that housed them, and became involved in racing as a mechanic at 17. His business was destroyed during World War II, and after the war he began building motorcycles.

In the following decades he moved into cars; his first was a roadster with a high-revving engine; the spiritual forebear of the S2000. Soichiro was an engineer first and a businessman second, and was on the verge of bankruptcy several times. But the ingenuity and quality of his engineering meant he ended up founding one of the world's greatest and most innovative automakers.

Buyers around the world have come to depend on their Hondas. By the late nineties the company also had a luxury brand—Acura—and a halo model in the fabulous NSX supercar, developed by the legendary Brazilian F1 driver Ayrton Senna. That car's sporting genes, together with Honda's hallmark engineering quality and reliability were put into a sports car we could all afford with the late 1990s release of the sporty S2000 roadster. It is constructed using a strong "X-bone" monocoque frame. It is lightweight, at 2,800 pounds, and has perfect 50/50 weight distribution front to rear. It has sexy, sharky styling and a screaming 8,000 rpm redline. Whatever you pay for it, you'll feel like you've paid far more.

**Above:** The CR—or Club Racer—is the epitomy of Honda capability, with firmer suspension, quicker steering ratio, and fully functional front and rear spoilers joining the aerodynamic design to increase rigidity and downforce and improve the overall driving experience.

**Left to right:** The roadster has been lightened from the original S2000, which has been accomplished partly by replacing the spare tire with a tire-repair kit and offering the audio system and air conditioning as options.

# Vehicle Design

From its earliest days, Honda went racing. The S2000 embodies this competitive spirit while also honoring the brand's racing history. 'The S2000 is a sports car designed by enthusiasts for enthusiasts,' says John Mendel, Executive Vice President of American Honda Motor Co., Inc. 'It raised the bar for all future roadsters, and it's already considered a classic by many Honda fans.'

The "CR"–for Club Racer–version of the S2000 is a final and fitting farewell for the nameplate. Like some other brands' lightweight specials, the CR is stripped down and enhanced for the track.

Though available as an option, the radio and air conditioning are removed. The car's soft-top, spare tire, and tools are completely deleted. A rear strut-tower brace takes some of the space vacated by the soft top to reinforce chassis stiffness. This and other strengthening measures make for a more rigid chassis, resulting in crisper handling.

Along with the GT-style wing at the back, a more aggressive front facia with a deep splitter, a bigger air intake, and winglets molded into the corners are big hints that this isn't an ordinary S2000. The interior features a black and yellow color combination with synthetic suede covering the seats.

**Top:** The highly-bolstered leather-trimmed seats are designed to cradle the driver and brace the body for quick maneuvers.

**Middle:** The cockpit has been fitted with left-hand audio controls and steering wheel-mounted cruise control, while the dashboard features digital panels.

**Bottom:** The gearshift is a spherical, aluminum knob.

# Performance

With zero-to-60 mph times in the mid-five-second range, few are going to take the S2000CR to the local dragstrip. But it is more than competitive judged against cars of similar price and purpose, and its low weight and revvy powerplant make it fun to hustle around just about any course.

Its relatively thin torque of 162lb-ft at a high 6,800 rpm indicates that this is an engine that needs to be worked vigorously, but taking it hard up through the gears is an addictive experience, particularly as the magnificent manual gearshift lets you fire off shifts with a quick flick of the wrist.

The CR is probably not the best choice for someone looking for a car that offers a calm, quiet weekend road trip with a loved one. Rather, it's for the hardcore car guy or girl who likes their car to have a bit of edge, and has something else in the garage—perhaps a standard S2000 with a roof—for daily duties.

## Jaguar XKR—A fast cat running with 510 horses

You might just be looking at the car that saved Jaguar. Before the new XK and supercharged XKR arrived in 2006, Jaguar was criticized for its staid, backward-looking styling, and the buyers were staying away. These cars were the first clean-sheet designs from Jaguar's new design director, Ian Callum.

Buyers and journalists alike loved them; they are elegant, modern and dynamic. They defined Jaguar's new look for its new, big-selling sedans, the XF and XJ, and got people excited about Jaguar again. And what's under those seductive lines is just as exciting.

Jaguar is one of many car brands with its origins in the motorcycle industry. Sir William Lyons was building motorcycle sidecars with a friend when they moved into automobile coach-building, releasing their first vehicles built atop an Austin chassis in 1935. He launched the legendary XK120 roadster at the 1948 Earls Court Motor Show, as the United Kingdom was recovering from the ravages of World War II. Not only was it a sporty car with graceful lines, but its 160-horsepower straight-six was an immensely powerful engine for the time. Only Cadillac was producing a more powerful engine in significant numbers and, for a time, the XK120 was the world's fastest production car. It was available in roadster and drophead coupé styles until the fixed-head coupé was added in 1951. Subsequent generations were designated XK140 and XK150, and production continued until 1961.

After decades of corporate ownership changes, Ford purchased the company in 1990 and held it until its sale in 2008 to India's Tata Motors. It was under Ford ownership that the XK was reborn in 1996. Buyers could select a coupé or convertible, as well as normally aspirated or supercharged V8 engines.

The all-new XK with its lightweight, all-aluminum monocoque chassis was released for the 2007 model year with output as high as 420 horsepower in supercharged XKR form. It was revised for 2010, with the XKR now boasting 510 horsepower. Only aircraft had that kind of power in 1948 when the first XK appeared.

**Above:** The XKR is powered by a supercharged five-liter V8 engine, with variable inlet camshaft phasing to develop 510 horsepower and a peak torque of 625 lb-ft; the car can accelerate from 0 to 60mph in 4.6 seconds. The supercharger maintains the same high levels of power at all engine speeds and provides instant response from the throttle as well as impressive mid-range acceleration.

**Left to right:** Twenty-inch Nevis alloy wheels, twin hood louvers and quad exhaust pipes are standard features, along with a new six-speed automatic transmission.

# Koenigsegg CCXR—Crushing the speed records

Sweden makes dull, safe, dependable cars. Italy does the outrageous supercars with unpronounceable names, right? Not entirely. In 1994 Sweden added a third automaker to Volvo and Saab, and it makes rather different cars. In 2005, a Koenigsegg CCR broke the McLaren F1's long-standing record as the world's fastest production car at a test at the Nardo high-speed circuit deep in southern Italy; home territory for its exotic rivals. Two other cars have since bested it, but Sweden's only sports car maker had finally arrived.

Christian von Koenigsegg's passion for cars began as a boy. He had a strong mechanical curiosity, and tuned cars as a teenager. But tuning wasn't enough; he wanted to build, from scratch, his own supercar, so he founded Koenigsegg at the age of 22.

Owning a supercar by that age would be impressive; starting your own supercar firm at 22, and creating a new model that bears your name, seems barely credible. He sketched the original design and two years later he had a prototype. His first client took delivery of his car at the Geneva Auto Show in 2002.

While many low-volume carmakers rely on other companies for their engines, Koenigsegg is almost unique in creating its own motor. The company also has its own production facility to fabricate many of its own lightweight alloy and carbon-fiber components.

The CCR that set the record "only" had 806 horsepower and 678 pound-feet of torque. The company launched the E85 bio-fuel-powered CCXR, with a Bugatti-beating 1,018 horsepower, in 2007. Just 25 will be made, but Koenigsegg announced an even more exclusive version, called the "Edition" with a target run of 20 units.

**Above:** The CCX maintains the distinctive shape of its predecessor, the CC, but has been designed with tighter lines and a more aggressive stance. The aerodynamic shape is award-winning and every aspect of the car has been designed for function and speed, avoiding unnecessary gadgets.

**Left to right:** The chassis is made of aluminum honeycomb with integrated fuel tanks designed to optimize safety and weight distribution. The front and rear suspensions are double wishbones with two-way adjustable VPS gas-hydraulic shock absorbers.

# Lamborghini Murciélago LP640—The bull keeps raging on

It all started with an argument. Ferruccio Lamborghini was a tractor maker and sports car lover from Sant'Agata Bolognese. He had a clutch problem in his Ferrari 250 GT, so he paid a visit to Enzo Ferrari at his headquarters in nearby Maranello. The car maker, who cared far more about racing cars than road cars and didn't care much at all about his customers, offended the tractor builder by suggesting that the problem lay with his driving. So the tractor maker decided to build his own sports cars.

The first Lamborghini—350 GTV—debuted at the Turin Motor Show in 1963, but it was the launch of the graceful and innovative Miura in 1966 that truly established Lamborghini, and frightened Ferrari. Dubbed P400 (for posteriori 4 litire), it had a 4-liter rear-mounted V12 with horsepower in the mid-300 range. The rear-mid-engine configuration was unique for a road car at the time, and many regard the Miura as the first supercar. This Murcielago LP640 traces its heritage back directly to the Miura.

The Miura was an elegant design with plenty of power. But the mighty Countach LP400—as on the LP640, "LP" means longitudinale posteriori, or rear engine positioned longitudinally front to rear—was an instant hit because of its outrageous, angular looks. Not only did it adorn the walls of young boys' bedrooms throughout the world in the 1970s and 1980s, it virtually trademarked scissor-style doors. Power was adequate for a supercar but not extreme, though later models (and especially its successor, the Diablo) upped the output considerably.

Ferruccio sold up in the 1970s, and ownership changed hands several times before the Volkswagen Group acquired Lamborghini in the late 1990s and introduced the 205 mile per hour Murciélago supercar at the 2001 Frankfurt Motor Show. The changes made to create the LP640 edition include even stronger performance, and an even wilder look.

**Above:** The LP640's tubular frame is made from high-strength steel alloy with carbon-fiber; the body is constructed from carbon-fiber and steel.

**Left to right:** The car's suspension is arranged in independent front and rear double wishbones, with anti-roll bars; its features include anti-dive and anti-squat The Lamborghini's brakes are power vacuum-assisted aluminum alloy calipers.

# Vehicle Design

Ferruccio was a Taurean and loved bulls, so Lamborghini model names typically refer to bulls or bullfighting and the company's logo is a raging bull. Murciélago is no exception; the word means a type of bat in Spanish, and was the name given to a famous Spanish fighting bull.

The bat reference made the Murciélago the obvious car of choice for Christian Bale's Bruce Wayne in the latest Batman films; it's only marginally less outrageous than the Batmobile he drives once in his black cape.

Parked next to the LP640, the original Murciélago looks downright naked, as virtually every intake and aerodynamic feature has grown to extreme proportions. Air intakes or vents are a significant and necessary design feature. The intakes atop the rear quarter panels rise at speed to feed more air to the engine, and the car is often displayed with these and the scissor doors raised, inspiring more spectator awe. Transparent glass above the engine is optional, and the car is available in coupé or roadster form.

Lamborghini describes the unique seat-stitching pattern, called Q-citura, in the LP640 as "lozenge-shaped", and changes to interior lighting and instrument panel graphics are part of the car's new look. As with most vehicles costing several hundred thousand dollars or Euros, the flagship Murciélago has virtually unlimited customization potential for clients willing to make an even bigger investment.

**Top:** Power-assisted rack and pinion steering comes as standard.

**Middle:** The clutch is a dry single plate with reduced pedal load.

**Bottom:** The car's transmission is permanent four-wheel drive, with a viscous traction system and electronic control system.

# Performance

The Ferrari-Lamborghini battle that began more than half century ago rages on, and in the ring this latest bull demands total respect. Its 6.5-liter rear-mid-mounted V12 pumps out 631 horsepower and nearly 500 pound-feet of torque—the "640" in the name is a reference to horsepower calculated to European standards. It is available with a stick-shift manual or optional E-Gear automated manual transmission driving all four wheels, and can sprint to 62 miles per hour in 3.4 seconds, or nearly half a second quicker than the original Murciélago.

A drive-by-wire system, along with variable valve timing, not only helps make horsepower, but makes the car slightly more user-friendly. In normal driving, 30 percent of power is transferred to the front axle, with the balance to the rear, but full power can be sent to the front or rear of the car to maintain traction and keep the car on course. The brakes have six-piston calipers and carbon ceramic brakes are optional. With more than 211 mph available, it's an option worth taking.

## At a Glance

**Country of manufacture**
Italy

**Engine**
Rear-mid-mounted V12 with aluminum block and heads, variable valve timing and drive-by-wire system.

| | |
|---|---|
| Displacement | 6.5 liter |
| Horsepower | 631 @ 8,000 rpm |
| Torque | 487 lb-ft @ 6,000 rpm |
| Rev limit | 8,000 rpm |

**Drivetrain**
6-speed manual or optional E-Gear; all-wheel drive.

**Suspension, handling, & braking**
Independent front and rear suspension with control arms, coil springs, and adjustable shocks; 6-piston brakes with carbon ceramic optional.

**Weights and measurements**

| | |
|---|---|
| Curb weight | 4,046 lbs |
| Wheelbase | 104.9 in |
| Length | 181.5 in |
| Width | 81.0 in |
| Height | 44.7 in |
| Track F/R | 64.4/66.7 in |
| Weight distribution | 42/58 |

**Performance**

| | |
|---|---|
| 0–62 (mfr est) | 3.4 sec |
| 0–100 mph | 8.0 sec |
| Quarter mile | 11.8 sec @ 124 mph |
| Top speed | >211 mph |
| Lateral grip | 0.96g |

# Lexus IS F—Putting the "F" in fun

The Lexus IS F has a specfication sheet you'll need to read twice, just to be sure you're not seeing things. Yes, this compact Japanese sedan really does have a five-liter, eight-cylinder engine with 416 horsepower and an eight-speed gearbox. Yes, it really will hit 60 mph in 4.6 seconds, and needs to be electronically limited to 170 mph. And all this from Lexus; a marque known until now for its quality, refinement, and luxury, and almost complete lack of sporting appeal. The IS-F might only be available as a four-door, but those incredible figures easily earn it inclusion in this collection of sports cars.

The idea for Toyota's luxury car brand was spawned in 1983 during a secret meeting of executives, when Chairman Eiji Toyoda challenged his team to create a car that could compete with the best in the world. Research and development began for a flagship, dubbed F1. The result was the LS400 full-size sedan shown at Detroit's 1989 North American International Auto Show.

Within a few years, the brand was selling globally, and to huge acclaim. With Lexus as a pioneer, other Japanese luxury brands, such as Infinity and Acura, invaded the United States. For generations, Ford and General Motors buyers could only aspire to poor-quality vehicles from Lincoln or Cadillac—and a limited number of European imports—when they could afford a premium brand. Suddenly, a generation that grew up relying on Japanese imports for transportation could upgrade to luxury cars from the brands that had already earned their trust.

Lexus launched a series of new models and added an entry-sized car to its ranks a decade after launch. Dubbed the IS, the front-engine, rear-drive sedan was intended as a not-so-subtle competitor to the BMW 3-Series and Mercedes C-Class. After several years of rumor and spy photos, the high-performance "F" performance version was announced in December 2006, and went on sale in 2008.

**Above:** The IS F was developed and tested on the Fuji Speedway and some of the most demanding racetracks in the world, The hand-built car can reach 62 mph in 4.8 seconds thanks to a 5.0-liter V8 engine.

**Left to right:** Formula 1 has heavily influenced the design of the car, from the race-tuned suspension and titanium intake valves to the powerful brakes and the contoured shape. The car boasts an upshift speed of just one-tenth of a second, one of the fastest available on the current market.

# Vehicle Design

The "F" in IS F and other Lexus vehicles that bear the performance designation refers to that first flagship F project at the company's inception, though some believe it also refers to Toyota's Fuji test track in Japan, where the F series cars are honed. Though the car obviously takes on BMW's M Series and Mercedes' AMG vehicles, Lexus denies targeting these competitors.

'The goal was to create a true performance sedan in a uniquely Lexus way—one that is totally authentic with a unique interpretation of raw driving thrill at all speeds and provides a whole new definition of "usable power",' explained Bob Carter, Group Vice President of Lexus Division.

The second-generation base-model IS was released in 2006, with luxury and power upgrades that widened the market beyond young enthusiasts. The F version starts with these changes and builds on an attractive design. Wider front fenders and grille, quad tailpipes, and a rear spoiler were a few of the exterior enhancements, along with a much-enlarged hood and lower intake that accommodates and cools the V8 engine.

The interior gets well-bolstered sport seats, as well as aluminized composite trim, and additional instrumentation. The difference is subtle, but clear, and the F badges are the real clue to what lies beneath.

**Top:** The interior systems can be operated using either voice or touch-screen and are placed on the Electro Multi-Vision VGA display.

**Middle:** The paddleshift lever is perforated leather with chrome inlay.

**Bottom:** The front seats are soft black semi-aniline leather, embossed with the logo of the IS F.

# Performance

Lexus might claim that the IS F wasn't intended to compete with any particular vehicle, but it seems an unlikely coincidence that the company just happened to shoehorn a V8 into its 3-Series rival, and get it to market just before the iconic M3 and with a fraction more power. That 416 horsepower lump sends power to the rear wheels through the world's first eight-speed automatic transmission, which boasts shift times as quick as Ferrari's F1 gearbox and is manually controlled with shift paddles behind the wheel.

The four-wheel independent suspension was lowered by more than an inch compared to standard IS models for better handling on track and street. It has a full complement of handling aids, but they have been recalibrated to allow more aggressive driving. The large Brembo brakes have six-piston calipers in front and two-piston calipers in the rear, and special mention must be made of the outrageously loud, rich V8 exhaust note. If you want evidence how completely Lexus has abandoned its obsession with whisper-quiet running in this car, just listen to it with the throttle wide open.

## At a Glance

**Country of manufacture**
Japan

**Engine**
Front-mounted, DOHC V8 with aluminum block and heads, four valves per cylinder, VVT-iE and VVT-i.

| | |
|---|---|
| Displacement | 5.0 liter |
| Horsepower | 416 @ 6,600 rpm |
| Torque | 371 lb-ft @ 5,200 rpm |
| Rev limit | 6,800 rpm |

**Drivetrain**
Eight-speed sport Direct-Shift automatic with paddle shifters and manual mode driving the rear wheels.

**Suspension, handling, & braking**
Independent front double-wishbone suspension with high-rate coil springs; independent rear multilink suspension with high-rate coil springs; stability and traction control systems, antilock brakes with Brembo 6-piston front calipers and 2-piston rear calipers.

**Weights and measurements**

| | |
|---|---|
| Curb weight | 3,780 lbs |
| Wheelbase | 107.5 in |
| Length | 183.5 in |
| Height | 55.7 in |
| Track F/R | 61.4/59.6 in |
| Weight distribution | 54/46 |

**Performance**

| | |
|---|---|
| 0–60 mph (mfr est). | 4.6 secs |
| Quarter mile | 13.0 |
| Top speed | 170 mph (governed) |

# Lotus Evora—Latest and greatest "E" car

Some sports cars share their badges with humble sedans churned out by the millions. Others come from start-up companies with no history of making road or racecars. But if you want your sports car to have real heritage, look no further than Lotus, and its latest model, the Evora.

It is impossible to discuss Lotus without mentioning its founder, the brilliant, mercurial, iconoclastic Colin Chapman. He experimented with several cars before launching the Lotus Seven in 1957, a design so timeless that they are still produced by Caterham in near-original form more than half a century later. Until his untimely death in 1982 at the age of 54, he helped engineer and oversaw the production of tens of thousands of successful race and street cars, and revolutionized the way both were conceived and built.

His racecars won the Formula 1 World Championship seven times, and his team's cadre of more than 40 drivers reads like a who's-who of motorsport: Mario Andretti, Graham Hill, Jim Clark, Emerson Fittipaldi, and more—and those are just the championship-winning drivers. Lotus clocked up 50 Grand Prix wins before Ferrari did, and won a total of 79. Other legends who competed in a Formula 1 with Lotus include Ayrton Senna, Jacky Ickx, Mika Häkkinen, and Alex Zanardi.

Lotus car names begin with an E because Chapman liked the sound of "Lotus Eleven". Iconic street cars that Lotus has produced include the Elite and Elan, along with the seminal, wedge-shaped Esprit. With seating for four, the Evora is the first mid-sized sports car from Lotus since the demise of the 28-year-old Esprit in 2004. It is also the first completely new model for Lotus in the dozen years since the Elise was launched. It's a very significant car, both for Lotus and for sports car enthusiasts everywhere.

**Above:** Featuring a modular, lightweight bonded aluminum structure, the chassis of the Lotus Evora includes a forged aluminum wishbone suspension, Bilstein high-performance dampers, and Eibach springs.

**Left to right:** The first product to be released from a five-year plan launched in 2006 to expand the range of Lotus cars, the Evora is a larger car than other recent Lotus models, weighing in at an estimated 2,976 lbs, and the only model to feature a 2+2 configuration, called the "Plus Zero" option.

# Vehicle Design

The Evora is that rarest of sports cars; a four-seater car with a mid-engine configuration. Other examples are Ferrari's 308GT4 and Mondial models; packaging an engine and a second row of seats within a sports cars wheelbase is difficult, but Lotus has managed it.

In addition to the extra seats, the attention paid to refinement and equipment options point to Lotus positioning the car as a premium coupé, unlike the raw, lightweight sports cars that have been the brand's hallmark until now. Another significant departure from tradition is that the cockpit has been designed for drivers taller than six feet, and can carry two sets of golf clubs in an air-conditioned trunk behind the engine.

Don't expect to get six-footers in the rear seats though; they're for children or short journeys only. But they give owners of Lotus's current two-seat Elise, Exige, and Europa models a reason to trade up once kids arrive, and it leaves room at the top of the range for the more extreme two-seat supercar Lotus is working on.

The car's sheet metal is unmistakably Lotus. 'The asymmetric wheel sizes, the short rear overhang, long front overhang, and cab-forward visor screen all contribute to giving the car visual movement and an agile stance,' explained Russell Carr, Lotus's Head of Design. 'This is incredibly important to us because we want the car's aesthetics to communicate its driving characteristics.'

**Top:** The hydraulically-assisted power steering is complemented by a six-speed manual gearbox.

**Middle:** The adjustable front seating is made from Recaro leather.

**Bottom:** Storage capacity includes a remote release glove box, storage bins and integrated cup holders, and a 160-liter boot.

# Performance

With a 276-horsepower V6 engine sourced from Toyota trying propel nearly 3,000 pounds, the Evora will be no sub-four-second scorcher. But the appeal of a Lotus always been about so much more than simple, straight-line speed. Much of the car world has turned to Lotus for suspension tuning, so handling is expected to be world-class. These are cars that breathe with the road, and manage to combine a silken ride with agile, intuitive handling. More power will come, but in standard form the Evora is no laggard; Lotus boasts that the car will lap Germany's tortuous Nürburgring race circuit faster than an Elise, has a zero-to-60 time under five seconds, and a top speed of about 160 miles per hour.

Those who like the car but want more power or a convertible should stay tuned. Lotus suggests that the chassis is good enough to remain in production for ten or more years, so expect a supercharged version with 350 horsepower or more and a drop-top version to arrive to keep us interested.

## At a Glance

**Country of manufacture**
United Kingdom

**Engine**
Lotus-tuned rear-mid DOHC V6 sourced from Toyota, with four valves per cylinder and dual VVT-i.

| | |
|---|---|
| Displacement | 3.5 liter |
| Horsepower | 276 @ 6,400 rpm |
| Torque | 252 lb-ft @ 4,700 rpm |
| Rev limit | 6,250 rpm |

**Drivetrain**
Choice of two 6-speed manual gearboxes, standard or close-ratio sport. Paddle-shifted automatic transmission in development.

**Suspension, handling, & braking**
Independent double forged aluminum wishbone suspension with Bilstein shock absorbers; stability and traction control systems; antilock brakes with AP Racing 4-piston calipers.

**Weights and measurements**

| | |
|---|---|
| Curb weight | 2,976 lbs |
| Wheelbase | 101.4 in |
| Length | 170.9 in |
| Width | 72.6 in |
| Height | 48.1 in |
| Track F/R | 61.6/61.3 in |
| Weight distribution | 39/61 |

**Performance**

| | |
|---|---|
| 0–60 mph (mfr est.) | <5 sec |
| Top speed (mfr est.) | 160 mph |
| FPA HWY Mileage | >30 mph |

# Maserati GranTurismo S—For a reality that trumps virtuality

Ferrari and Maserati are both controlled by Italian car giant Fiat Automobiles, and the way they share their technology is something of a double-edged sword. Maserati owners get to boast that their car is engineered with legendary Ferrari technology, while Ferrari owners have to concede that the technology in their car may be available in a less-expensive Maserati version.

Family rivalry aside, the gorgeous Maserati GranTurismo S is one of the most well-rounded sports cars in production. Not only is it striking to look at, but its 433 horsepower engine and sport-tuned suspension have both been upgraded from the standard GranTurismo, itself a major improvement over the model it replaced in 2008. Add this car's looks to its performance and heritage and lucky owners won't need to call on the Ferrari associations to make their car seem more exciting or desirable.

Maserati's heritage dates back more than 80 years. The company was founded in Bologna, Italy, by the Maserati brothers—Alfieri, Carlo, Bindo, Mario, Ettore, and Ernesto. With Alfieri at the wheel, the fledgling manufacturer achieved its first win in the legendary Targa Florio, a gruelling road race through Sicily. The company was relocated to Modena, just 30 minutes from then-rival Ferrari, and at the heart of Italy's Supercar Valley; Lamborghini and now Pagani are also near-neighbours. More racing success followed, including back-to-back Indianapolis 500 victories in 1939 and 1940, and numerous Grand Prix wins in the 1950s with legendary drivers Sir Stirling Moss and Juan Manuel Fangio. An Argentine native, Fangio is arguably the greatest Formula 1 driver of all time.

Maserati's street car sales grew with the win count; road cars like this GranTurismo can call on a solid-gold sporting heritage that few other makes can match. But, like other Italian sports car makers, Maserati suffered from labour disputes, poor quality and reliability, and the effects of recessions and oil crises on its high-priced offerings. But it found stability in its partnership with Fiat and Ferrari from the 1990s, allowing it to launch a welcome global comeback.

**Above:** The GranTurismo S was designed to be aggressive, a look achieved through a combination of the new shape given to the side spoilers and the rear spoiler that has been fully integrated into the bootlid. Both features also add to the aerodynamic efficiency of the model, the side spoilers directing the airflow towards the rear wheels while the rear spoiler improves downforce.

**Left to right:** The Trident symbol, as well as the oval "Saetta" logo, are featured on the front grille and rear pillars, the red prongs of the trident echoing the color of the standard brake callipers.

# Vehicle Design

The GranTurismo (Italian for Grand Touring) made its world debut in 2007 at the Geneva International Motor Show, with the "S" version appearing a year later. Maserati describes the visual theme of its cars as "dynamic elegance", and asked the fabled Italian design studio Pininfarina to create a fluid look for its new model that would still be recognizable without the famous Trident badge.

Maserati vehicles of recent decades have lacked a clear visual identity so, for this car, Pininfarina reached right back to the 1950s and 60s for inspiration. Jason Castriota, Pininfarina's Exterior Designer, explained that cars from that era had strong character that defined the brand, but also that the firm wanted a timeless car that would age well and that didn't slavishly follow the past.

Design changes for the "S" include a menacing black grille, red brake calipers, and red accents on the Trident logos, as well as enhanced rocker panels and an integrated spoiler on the trunk lid.

Interior trim options in the relatively large four-seat coupé include leather from acclaimed supplier Poltrona Frau, which supplies many other sports and supercar makers, and the racier Alcantara suede-effect fabric. As with other high-end Italian sports cars, an extensive personalization program is offered.

**Top:** The central zone of the seats are finished in Alcantara and horizontal piping.

**Middle:** The GranTurismo S features seven-spoke 20-inch rims featuring stylized Tridents.

**Bottom:** The chrome-edged gear shift paddles are mounted behind the steering wheel, while the central console features a panel for the first and reverse gear switches through an electro-actuated gearbox.

# Performance

With a respectable 433 horsepower on tap, 60 miles per hour comes up in 4.8 seconds or better, with a quarter-mile time of 13.0 seconds. But you have to work the engine relatively hard to produce those figures; peak power arrives at 7,000 rpm, and the peak torque of 361 lb-ft is relatively thin, particularly by comparison with this car's turbocharged or supercharged rivals.

But the wail produced as the revs rise is unmistakable, unforgettable, and utterly addictive; revving it to the redline is hardly a chore. The exhaust system features pneumatic valves that open when "Sport" mode is engaged to give the car much more volume. The MC-Shift electro-actuated gearbox can be used in automatic or manual mode with paddle shifters.

Handling has been tightened up by comparison with the standard GranTurismo, with crisper turning and braking to match the 18-horsepower increase. And you get to share it all with three friends; who needs a Ferrari?

## At a Glance

**Country of manufacture**
Italy

**Engine**
Front-mid DOHC V8 with 4 valves per cylinder and variable valve timing.

| | |
|---|---|
| Displacement | 4.7 liter |
| Horsepower | 433 @ 7,000 rpm |
| Torque | 361 lb-ft @ 4,700 rpm |
| Rev limit | 7,600 rpm |

**Drivetrain**
Graziano 6-speed rear transaxle with MC-Shift electro-actuated gearbox and paddle shifters; shifts in 100 ms.

**Suspension, handling, & braking**
Independent front and rear double-wishbone suspension (Skyhook adjustable system is optional); stability and traction control systems; front Brembo-sourced front brakes have dual-cast iron/aluminum discs gripped by six-piston aluminum calipers.

**Weights and measurements**

| | |
|---|---|
| Curb weight | 4,146 lbs |
| Wheelbase | 115.8 in |
| Length | 192.2 in |
| Width | 75.4 in |
| Height | 53.3 in |
| Track F/R | 61.9/63.0 in |
| Weight distribution | 47/53 |

**Performance**

| | |
|---|---|
| 0–60 mph (mfr est.) | 4.8 sec |
| Quarter mile (mfr est.) | 13.0 sec |

# Mercedes-Benz SL65 AMG Black Series— Black is the new "really fast"

In the world of absolutes and ultimates, people with the best are well aware when something new and even better comes along. And so it is in the world of AMG, the in-house tuning arm of Mercedes-Benz renowned for its thunderous makeovers of Merc's standard cars. Owners of the "regular" SL65—one of several AMG versions of Merc's elegant SL sports car—with "only" 604 horsepower no longer have baddest Benz on the block. That title now belongs to the SL65 AMG Black Series, with its 612 horsepower and dramatically different bodywork.

The "Black" treatment is a step above AMG's usual, very complete overhaul. Even seasoned racecar drivers were wowed by the structural enhancements to the smaller CLK63 Black, and the dramatic impact the changes had on its handling. For the SL65 Black, the usual folding hardtop has been replaced with a fixed carbon-fiber roof, which increases torsional stiffness to the benefit of handling, and reduces weight to the benefit of performance. In total, more than 500 pounds were shed with the use of lightweight materials. Add to that a wider track, bigger brakes, and enhanced dynamics, and the result is a bruiser of a car that can make it around Germany's tough Nürburgring circuit at least as quickly as Merc's McLaren-developed SLR hypercar.

More power and less weight means zero-to-60 times are likely to be at least a few ticks quicker than the regular SL65 AMG. The factory rating on the Black Series is 4.2 seconds, but consensus is that it will be quicker than that. But wealthy Black Series owners are unlikely to be found setting quarter-mile times at the local dragstrip. In fact, they don't need to drive at all to let people know just how fast this car is; its outrageous wide-body looks alone get the message across. And only one year of production, strictly limited to 350 units, means this car's extraordinary street presence is unlikely to be equalled, let alone upstaged.

**Above:** The SL65 AMG houses the most powerful AMG engine to have been developed to date. The supercharged V12 has a 6-liter capacity and allows the car to reach 62 mph in 4.2 seconds with 612 horsepower.

**Left to right:** The sporty look of the SL65 AMG has been enhanced from previous models, with new AMG bodystyling, and features that include unique design contours on the hood, an AMG spoiler lip, and 19-inch AMG light-alloy wheels in a twin-spoke design.

# Vehicle Design

The price difference between the regular SL65 and the Black Series is large enough to purchase a SL550, or take a few world cruises. Cynics may question whether the extra performance merits the increase in cost, but the looks alone are priceless. All the body panels except the doors were replaced with lightweight carbon-fiber pieces, and the extra-wide fenders lend the car an extraordinarily muscular stance.

The front air intake and splitter have grown to massive proportions, with cooling vents atop the hood and ports behind the front wheels; this car has a lot of heat to dissipate. These modifications, along with the reshaped hardtop, give the car a more sporting character than the convertible SL.

AMG boss Thomas Rappel said, during a sneak peek at the New York Auto Show, that the folding roof was also eliminated because it didn't fit between the massive 325-section rear tires, and the goal was a very different look to the standard SL. 'We wanted it to look more like a proper coupé,' he added.

From the rear, the stock tail lamps remain, but dual trapezoidal tailpipes, a lip spoiler that rises into a wing, and those dragster-esque tires more than a foot wide set it apart from lesser SLs.

**Top:** The Cockpit Management and Navigation Display, or COMAND, includes a 6.5-inch color display, radio, hard disk drive, map navigation system, and Linguatronic voice control.

**Middle:** The multi-contoured seating features backrests with massage function as well as being electronically adjustable with memory and heating.

**Bottom:** The V12 logo features prominently on the exterior of the car.

# Performance

The big news under the hood is the bump in power, courtesy of the increased size of the twin turbochargers. Mercedes claims that the potential peak torque output is nearly 1,000 pound-feet, but that it had to be limited to the regular SL65's 738 pound-feet to protect the rest of the drivetrain. That monstrous torque figure is already too much for the company's seven-speed transmission to handle, so the five-speed automatic with paddle shifters is again tapped for duty, reprogrammed for performance use with special four-mode Speedshift software.

Like the other cars in the Black Series family, camber curves, wheel alignment, and shock damping rates are all adjustable, and the chassis has been strengthened for improved handling.

But perhaps the greatest performance difference between the Black Series and other SLs is the speed limit. The Black Series can wind all the way up to 199 miles per hour, rather than the 155-mile-per-hour cap imposed on humbler Mercs. If you have the very best, why impose any limits?

## At a Glance

**Country of manufacture**
Germany

**Engine**
Front-mounted, twin-turbocharged DOHC 12-cylinder engine with 3 valves per cylinder.

| | |
|---|---|
| Displacement | 6.0 liter |
| Horsepower | 612 @ 4,800 rpm |
| Torque | 1,000 lb-ft @ 2,000-4000 rpm |
| Rev limit | 5,950 rpm |

**Drivetrain**
5-speed AMG Speedshift Plus automatic driving rear wheels.

**Suspension, handling, & braking**
Independent front suspension

**Weights and measurements**

| | |
|---|---|
| Curb weight | 2,120 lbs |
| Wheelbase | 100.8 in |
| Length | 180.7 in |
| Width | 77.2 in |
| Height | 51.6 in |

**Performance**

| | |
|---|---|
| 0–60 mph (mfr est.) | 4.2 sec |
| Top speed | 199 mph |

**Trivia**
Each AMG engine is hand-built, using a "one man, one engine" philosophy, at the current AMG plant in Affalterbach, Germany, and each of these engines has a plaque with the engine builder's signature.

# Mercedes-Benz SLR McLaren 722 Edition— Sport, Leicht, Rennsport

This car simply drips with racing pedigree. It's all there in the name. Mercedes-Benz and McLaren each have an extraordinary history in motorsport, and now compete together at the very top level of Formula 1. AMG, Mercedes' in-house tuning arm, builds awesome road cars based on Merc's standard models but itself has a fine independent racing pedigree.

SLR stands for Sport, Light, Racing; after a series of Mercedes-Benz racecars. And arguably the greatest was the 300SLR bearing the number 722, which Sir Stirling Moss drove to victory in the 1955 Mille Miglia. The number emblazoned on the hood stood for his 7:22 start time. He completed the thousand-mile Italian road race in just over ten hours, averaging nearly 100 mph and at times touching 170 mph; all this with 1950s technology, and on 1950s Italian public roads. The race was deemed too dangerous two years later and was outlawed; Moss's record still stands and it remains one of the greatest drives in motorsport.

McLaren traces its origins to the race team that racing star Bruce McLaren started in 1963. McLaren, a New Zealander, began racing at age 14 and, age 22, became the youngest Formula 1 winner to that point with his victory in the 1959 United States Grand Prix. Prior to his tragic death in a severe crash at 32, he had four wins and 27 podium finishes in Formula 1 and Can-Am sports car competition. Racecars campaigned by the company he founded have won the Indianapolis 500 three times, as well as victories in the 24 Hours of Le Mans and 12 Hours of Sebring. And, at its first attempt, McLaren made arguably the greatest road car in the world with the McLaren F1.

Collaboration on the Mercedes-Benz SLR McLaren began in 1999 and was led by the legendary engineer Gordon Murray, creator of the F1.

**Above:** Designed as much to be a piece of automotive art as an impressive sports car, the SLR McLaren Roadster takes many of its styling cues from the SLRs of the 1950s and merges them with the advanced aerodynamics and sophistication of Formula 1 cars.

**Left to right:** The model's features of note include the front spoiler, designed to be assertive, the air vents in the wings, exhaust pipes intended to catch the eye, the compact tail, and the dihedral doors.

# Vehicle Design

The modern SLR is true to the original formula: a two-seat sports car with a strong engine housed in a long nose, with short front and rear overhangs and side vents. There was long internal debate about whether the car should be configured with the engine in front—like the 300SLR and all Mercedes street cars—or amidships, like the McLaren Formula 1 racecar and F1 road car. The front-mid engine layout was chosen. The Vision SLR concept was unveiled by Mercedes in 1999, with deliveries of the production SLR starting in 2004. The 722 edition was released in 2006.

While the fixed-roof 300SLR had gullwing doors, the SLR McLaren impresses curbside with its equally exotic scissor doors, and the long, raised center section of the hood is suggestive of its Formula 1 lineage. The 722 edition differs from the original with a modified front spoiler and air splitter, rear diffuser, and special badging. A grippier racing steering wheel with hunting-leather lining, gearshift paddles, and black carbon highlights hint at its racing inspiration.

In addition to the 722, other variants include a roadster, the track-only 722 GT, and a lightweight speedster final edition named after Sir Stirling Moss.

**Top:** Black Alcantara has been used to finish the seats, insides of the doors, and roof liner, mixed with leather to achieve a distinctive look.

**Middle:** The headlamp surrounds are in palladium gray.

**Bottom:** The sports steering wheel is trimmed in black suede for ease of grip, the same material featuring on the handbrake lever, gear knob, and inside door handles.

# Performance

Steffen Köhl and Gorden Wagener handled the SLR's styling, while Gordon Murray oversaw the SLR's engineering. The car suffered from an identity crisis. Many critics saw it as a grand tourer rather than a sports car due to its five-speed automatic transmission and 3,801-pound curb weight.

Semantics and drivetrain notwithstanding, the SLR had outrageous performance. The 722 edition hits the streets with a supercharged 5.5-liter V8 handbuilt in AMG's clinical workshop in Affalterbach, Germany. It pumps out 641 horsepower and 780 pound-feet of torque, good for zero-to-60 times in the mid-three-second range and a top speed of almost 210 miles per hour.

The 722 edition has stiffer suspension with lower ride height for improved handling. Like the original SLR, it has a rear spoiler that, if activated, can pop up like an air brake to help slow the car. Given the performance and the cost of replacing the panels, we're sure that owners find this feature particularly reassuring.

# At a Glance

**Country of manufacture**
United Kingdom

**Engine**
Front-mounted, supercharged 5.5-liter DOHC V8.

| | |
|---|---|
| Displacement | 5.5 liter |
| Horsepower | 641 @ 6,200 rpm |
| Torque | 780 lb-ft @ 3,250–5,000 rpm |

**Drivetrain**
5-speed automatic transmission.

**Suspension, handling, & braking**
Independent front and rear suspension, traction and stability systems, antilock brakes.

**Weights and measurements**

| | |
|---|---|
| Curb weight | 3,801 lbs |
| Wheelbase | 106.3 in |
| Length | 183.3 in |
| Width | 75.1 in |
| Height | 49.6 in |
| Track F/R | 61.9/63.0 in |
| Weight distribution | 50/50 |

**Performance**

| | |
|---|---|
| 0–62 (mfr est.) | 3.6 sec |
| Top speed (mfr est.) | 209 mph |

**Trivia**
Renowned car collector, Jay Leno, claims to have put more miles on his SLR than any supercar in his garage.

A replacement caliper for the SLR costs about $15,000 US.

# Mosler MT900S—Built to overtake the big dogs

It's a classic sports car formula: take an extremely light and agile chassis and just cram in as much horsepower as possible. This simple, effective theory has defined Warren Mosler's car-building career. Mosler, a prosperous multi-billion-dollar hedge fund manager who engineered and built cars on the side, launched his first car in the mid-1980s. Called the Consulier GTP, it wasn't the most attractive car, but it was fast, with a one-ton curb weight and 2.2-liter turbocharged Chrysler engine. Cars from Consulier, and its subsequent spin-off Mosler Automotive, have competed and won on tracks throughout the world, including enough One Lap of America events during the 1990s to be banned—twice.

The Florida-based company named its all-new Mosler MT900 after Mosler's initial and that of designer Rob Trenne, who had previously worked on the C5 Corvette. The "900" designation represents the vehicle's very ambitious target weight in kilograms, and the 2,200-pound curb weight of the updated MT900S shows it didn't miss by much.

It took Mosler several years to get the MT900S through all the rigorous testing required to earn a car street-legal status in the United States. It was finally certified in 2005 and deliveries began in 2006. In the meantime, more than a dozen competition cars were built and sold, both in the United States and in Europe. The cars achieved victory on the track on both sides of the Atlantic, most notably a class win in the 2003 24 Hours of Daytona endurance classic.

The MT900 was powered by a basic C5 Corvette LS1 engine, while the newer "S" variant received a significant horsepower boost with the installation of a supercharged LS6 from the Z06. This upgrade put it squarely into supercar territory, with a round 600 horsepower and 557 pound-feet of torque.

**Above:** The MT900S has been designed as a long-distance Grand Tourer with all the features of a sportscar, from the high speed to the comfort. It boasts a high power-to-weight ratio, a low front, and an efficient aerodynamic design.

**Left to right:** The car is capable of reaching 60 mph in just 3.4 seconds and 100 mph in 7.5 seconds, with a maximum speed of 190 mph and over. The chassis is carbon composite with double-wishbone, alloy upright suspension at both the front and rear ends.

# Vehicle Design

Extensive use of carbon-fiber and Kevlar composite materials keep the Moslers at fighting weight. Using extreme mass-reduction techniques to achieve outrageous performance in a street-legal car brings a trade-off; the result feels—and sounds—like a hardcore track car. But that's exactly why some buyers will choose it.

At first glance, the MT9000S is not unlike a Saleen S7, with its long tail, but closer observation reveals a unique design worthy of garage posters. The lines of the car are flowing and simple, with vented fenders and an elongated oval air channel that serves as both an air outlet from the front of the car and intake for the engine.

'We designed the MT900S to be an extreme performance vehicle,' says Mosler. 'The MT900S is intended as the ultimate road-going street car for a discriminating group of enthusiasts, collectors, and investors capable of appreciating its performance to the fullest.'

The interior is adequate, if not luxurious, with several components that look understandably borrowed from the parts bin of engine supplier, General Motors. Power steering adds weight so it isn't included, though the car's low mass means it's not like driving an old truck.

Despite its all-American image and engine, final assembly of the Mosler is handled in the United Kingdom by Breckland, manufacturer of the Biera.

**Top:** Sparco Evo race seats with a four-point race harness, with full leather or Alacantara trim, are optional on the MT900S, as well as a Sparco flat-bottom steering wheel.

**Middle:** The tires are Michelin Pilot Sport PS2, complemented by a 109-inch wheelbase.

**Bottom:** The MT900S features electro-hydraulic assisted R&P steering with six gears, not including reverse.

# Performance

Some cars look fast and fail to deliver, but the MT900S delivers performance to match its appearance. The 600 horsepower from the rear-mid engine is delivered to the rear wheels through a Porsche-sourced six-speed manual gearbox. Many top-flight supercars weigh a quarter of a ton more than the race-bred MT900S, and more still in some cases.

But big power and low weight mean this dramatic package can sprint to 60 miles per hour in a paltry 3.1 seconds, faster than supercars from many of the world's established brands. Eleven-second quarter-mile runs at 135 miles per hour and 6.5 seconds to 100 miles per hour are the kind of performance numbers you'd expect of hypercars costing far more.

These staggering numbers don't come at the expense of handling, either; the Mosler generates 1.08g of lateral grip. Don't look for electronic aids, but with huge grip and little mass transfer, drivers will have to work hard to find the limits of adhesion. Expect to be travelling very, very fast when you do.

## At a Glance

**Country of manufacture**
United States/United Kingdom

**Engine**
Rear-mid supercharged pushrod General Motors LS6 V8 with 2 valves per cylinder, aluminum block and heads.

| | |
|---|---|
| Displacement | 5.4 liter |
| Horsepower | 600 @ 6,300 rpm |
| Torque | 557lb-ft @ 4,000 rpm |
| Boost | 6 psi/0.41 bar |
| Rev limit | 6,500 rpm |

**Drivetrain**
6-speed manual gearbox.

**Suspension, handling, & braking**
Independent front and rear suspension, vented disc brakes.

**Weights and measurements**

| | |
|---|---|
| Curb weight | 2,200 lbs |
| Wheelbase | 109.0 in |
| Length | 189.0 in |
| Width | 79.0 in |
| Height | 43.5 in |
| Track F/R | 66.0/66.0 in |

**Performance**

| | |
|---|---|
| 0–60 mph | 3.1 sec |
| 0–100 mph | 6.5 sec |
| Quarter mile | 11.0 sec @ 135 mph |
| Top speed (mfr est.) | >190 mph |

**Trivia**
*Star Wars* producer and director, George Lucas, took delivery of the first street legal MT900S, a black car with black interior.

# Nissan 370Z—The amazing Fairlady

Japan's reputation for producing dull cars is entirely undeserved. Sure, the majority of its output might be staid Camrys and Corollas, but occasionally it makes a sports car good enough to win a cult following around the globe and lure buyers away from even the most aspirational European brands.

The Nissan-Datsun 240Z was one such car. Launched in 1970 and known as the Fairlady in Japan after an earlier Nissan roadster, it emulated the look of popular European sports cars from the likes of Jaguar and Ferrari, and had a gutsy 2.4-liter inline four-cylinder engine that revved to 7,000 rpm and generated 146 horsepower. As emissions restrictions strangled many cars, subsequent "Z" cars often produced more horsepower than many V8 engines as the model developed throughout the 1970s and 80s.

During the 1990s, the 300ZX was the darling of the motoring press, earning numerous awards prior to the end of production in 1996. Sports car fans eagerly awaited its return, and the "Z" badge was revived with the launch of the 350Z in 2002. It was released at the same time as the upmarket Infinity G35; the vehicles share Nissan's FM platform—for front-midship engine—with the ferocious and fine-handling GT-R.

Nissan automobiles can trace their roots back far further than most Japanese carmakers, and all the way to 1914, when Kwaishinsha Motorcar Works launched the first DAT. By the 1930s, the company had been absorbed into corporate conglomerate, Nissan. DAT has been producing a small car, named Datson, which was renamed Datsun. Manufacturing agreements after World War II allowed Nissan to replicate Austin vehicles from the United Kingdom. This technology evolved into the engine that powered the small, Datsun-branded 510 sedan, which helped earn the company worldwide recognition. Nissan finally killed the Datsun brand in the 1980s, and in the 1990s it formed an alliance with French carmaker Renault.

**Above:** The 370Z's suspension was honed and tested at the Nürburgring. Its front-engined design with rear wheel drive focuses on the power-to-weight ratio of the car, the V6 3.7 liter engine, with variable valve timing and lift, pushing the car to 60 mph in 5.1 seconds, with 270 lb-ft of torque.

**Left to right:** Boomerang tail lights are one aspect of the aggressive classic Z design that has been retained for the 370Z. The 370Z also features lightweight aluminum-alloy double-wishbone suspension.

# Nissan GT-R—Godzilla has escaped from Tokyo

The 3.8-liter V6-powered Nissan GT-R doesn't look like a rival for Ferraris and Lamborghinis with eight and ten cylinders, and Nissan's brand image is certainly no match. But the GT-R has desirability and performance that transcend its blue-collar badge. Officially it produces 480 hp, but the engines are expensively hand-finished and independent dyno tests have revealed power outputs well in excess of that.

The figures prove it has the performance. The desirability comes from the fact that Nissan has produced a car that is not only a technological marvel, and therefore desirable in the same way as high-end hi-fi or a Swiss watch with myriad complications, but also intoxicatingly exciting to drive.

Skyline GT-Rs were first marketed from 1969 to 1977. In 1989, the name was revived with the R32, which dominated Japanese and Australian motorsports with its twin-turbo inline-six cylinder engine and ATTESA-ETS all-wheel drive system. This car's performance earned it the "Godzilla" nickname. These earlier generation GT-Rs often looked like little more than plain coupés with flared fenders and bolt-on ground effects, but their performance became known—and desired—worldwide. The R33 version was the first production car with a sub-eight-minute lap at the legendary Nürburgring circuit in Germany. Production ceased in 2002 with the R34, by when Skyline GT-Rs were generating somewhere around 325 horsepower, though they were "officially" rated at 276 horsepower in accordance with Japanese government limits.

Concepts hinting at the new generation GT-R appeared at the Tokyo Motor Show in 2001 and 2005, with the production version making its debut there in 2007. In that six-year timeframe, excitement for the next generation grew to a frenzy. By the end of 2008, customers in Europe and America were taking finally taking delivery. Godzilla was back, and those exotic brands were preparing to be embarrassed.

**Above:** The GT-R contains a 3.8-liter twin-turbocharged 24-valve V6, each engine created by a single master technician in a clean-room environment. The horsepower of the engine is 480 and the car's top speed is 193 mph.

**Left to right:** The car's hood, trunk lid, and outer door skins are aluminum, with die-cast aluminum front shock towers and door structures. The outer body panels are stamped with a multiple-strike coining process to ensure exceptional rigidity and precision.

# Pagani Zonda F—Combining Italian flair with German power

Every year brings a fresh crop of would-be supercar makers. Most produce a concept car. Some make—and even sell—a few driveable examples of their car. But almost all fail, crippled by the huge costs involved in developing a supercar to the sky-high standards set by the most demanding buyers in the world, and by the established and well-funded supercar makers.

Pagani is a rare exception. Not only has it created and successfully sold a new supercar, but it has created one with the visual flair and build quality and performance to embarrass those established players. Italy's Supercar Valley has a new resident, and this one is here to stay.

Founder Horacio Pagani is an Argentine-born Italian who began sculpting supercars from wood and clay at 12 years old. After becoming a racecar designer as a young man, he met and befriended the legendary Argentine Formula 1 driver Juan Manuel Fangio. Pagani moved to Italy, worked in Lamborghini's composite department and founded his own firm in 1988. His company worked with Lamborghini on several projects before he created a prototype he had designed a few years earlier. The car was named the Fangio F1 as a tribute to his friend and, during the mid-1990s, Fangio helped again with an introduction to Mercedes, who agreed to supply engines for the project.

After Fangio passed away, Pagani changed the name to the C12 Zonda to avoid capitalizing on his friend's famous name when he presented the car at the 1999 Geneva Auto Show. The alphanumeric designation is from the first initial of his wife, Christina, combined with the number of cylinders. The car is powered by the Mercedes-Benz M120 V12 engine used in, among others models, the S-Class sedan. The performance it generates in the Zonda is rather more impressive.

**Above:** The Zonda F is powered by a Mercedes-Benz engine in honor of Juan Manuel Fangio, who upheld the opinion while enthusiastically following the car's development program that it needed to be innovative, safe, and powered by Mercedes-Benz.

**Left to right:** The 12-cylinder V60° AMG engine has 48 valves and a displacement of 7291 cc. The intake manifold is aluminum hydroformed alloy while the exhaust is hydroformed steel and ceramic coated, inconel manifold, titanium muffler.

# Vehicle Design

The more powerful "F" version of the C12 Zonda—finally honoring Fangio—was launched at the 2005 Geneva Auto Show. The Zonda looks every bit the closed-cockpit racecar. Many of the changes to the F were hidden structural improvements, while visible changes include a revised front end, a new rear spoiler, and more vents.

The interior is one of the most creative and original of any car. The instrument cluster has a polished metal surround that looks like it was designed by a jeweller, while a red starter button sits atop the gearshift, prompting the driver to awaken the beast. Prospective clients may wish to opt for a carbon-fiber interior, and avoid the wood accents on the show car, which are finely crafted but can seem out of place.

As exotic as the whole package is, probably the most spectacular view is from the rear, which is simply like no other. Massive upper and lower spoilers sandwich a mesh air vent grille that has a circular enclosure with quad exhaust tips. Round tail lamps are stacked vertically on either side; the design would look at home on a spaceship.

**Top:** The Zonda F is a longitudinal mid-engine car with rear wheel drive.

**Middle:** The car boasts a twin-plate clutch and mechanical six-speed gearbox.

**Bottom:** The steering is TRW rack and pinion assisted, with a hydraulic power brakes and four ventilated Brembo disks.

## Performance

Aerodynamics may keep the Zonda out of the 250 mile-per-hour club, and the absence of an all-wheel drive system means it won't generate enough traction to produce a sub-three-second zero-to-60 time. But how often do you floor your car from standstill, or take it to its V-max? In real-world driving, the Zonda F is undeniably one of the fastest and most outrageous sports cars you can buy. The Clubsport version has set the Nürburgring record not once, but twice. The first time it dethroned the Porsche Carrera GT, with the second record coming in 2008. The Maserati MC12 and Dodge Viper SRT-10 ACR are the only cars to have bettered the time so far.

A 3.6-second zero-to-60 time, 220 mile-per-hour top speed, and especially its 1.4g lateral grip, are impressive by any standard, and an even more outrageous "R" track version has been announced that borrows the engine from the Mercedes CLK-GTR competition car. It will doubtless be a blast to drive. But the F will probably remain the best Zonda; devastatingly fast, fascinating to behold, and remarkably civilized for such a titan.

# Panoz Esperante GTLM—Race breeding for the street

On June 18, 2006, father and son team, Don and Dan Panoz, were finally able to pop the cork on a bottle of champagne to celebrate their class win in the demanding 24 Hours of Le Mans. It was an achievement more than a decade in the making.

'The dream of winning here lives inside anyone who has entered Le Mans,' said Don. 'The greatest manufacturers in the world—Porsche, Audi, BMW, Ferrari, and countless others—have been victorious at Le Mans and as a result are part of history. I can't begin to describe how proud and satisfied I am to see the Panoz brand alongside these elite names.'

The son of an Italian immigrant to the United States, Don Panoz founded two pharmaceutical companies, the second of which was established in Ireland and holds the worldwide patent for the nicotine patch. While Don built his business there, son Dan worked at Thompson Motor Company, which manufactured cars. He purchased the rights to one of the chassis when the company closed and started the Panoz Automotive Development Company.

Based in northern Georgia, they released a Ford V8-powered Roadster in 1990. Convinced that his son's road cars would have more success with a racing pedigree, father Don created the race team while Dan saw to the production car program. Along the way, they purchased three major racetracks (Sebring, Road America, and Mosport) and launched their own championship, the American Le Mans Series.

Over the course of ten years, Panoz competed in the ALMS and traveled across the Atlantic to do battle in the epic 24 Hours of Le Mans every year—first in prototype racecars, and then in the GT class with a race version of the Esperante GTLM coupé. They were finally able to bring home victories from both the 12 Hours of Sebring and the holy grail of endurance racing, Le Mans. What they l earnt in those races, and the credibility created by their victories, is carried over to their mighty road cars.

**Above:** The Esperante GTLM has been designed to merge race-inspired design with American muscle power, combining a supercharged, inter-cooled 4.6L V8, 32-valve engine, hand assembled, with a six-speed manual transmission.

**Left to right:** With sequential electronic fuel injection and a Tremec 156 six-speed manual transmission, the car has a 4.6-liter displacement and a limited-slip differential, delivering world class performance.

# Porsche 911 GT3 RS—Summoning the spirit of the original 911

The Porsche 911 is the definitive, benchmark sports car. Fans of Ferrari and the other sports car makers who have battled Porsche on road and track for decades may disagree, and the rear-engined layout which the 911 has stuck with since its launch in 1964, might be illogical and bad for handling. But critics and cynics can't argue with the fact that, for nearly half a century, the 911 has been the point of reference for judging new sports cars of a similar price. It's very rare for a new rival to be considered better, and the experts testing for car magazines still regularly prefer the 911 to sports cars costing far more.

But how would you like your 911? From the basic Carrera to the terrifying GT2, the 911 is a range within a range, spanning a broad spectrum of price, power, and bodystyle. But for people who really know 911s, one version stands out. The GT3 still delivers the edgy, almost dangerous thrill that used to mark a 911, and the yet-more extreme RS version magnifies that further.

Porsche's heritage begins virtually at the dawn of the automobile. Dr Ferdinand Porsche was building cars before the turn of the last century. Without a formal education, he became a respected automotive engineer and is known best for his creation of the Volkswagen Beetle. His son Ferry was equally talented. When he couldn't find a car he was happy with, he developed what became the Porsche 356, and he sold pre-orders to prospective dealers door-to-door until he had enough cash for his first run in 1948. Early versions of the little roadster and subsequent coupé housed Volkswagen mechanicals until Porsche was able to re-engineer the components with its own technology. Thus, the tradition of air-cooled, rear-engine, rear-drive sports cars began.

The 356 was replaced in 1964 by the 911, which retains the same basic shape even today. The 911 has earned victories virtually everywhere a sports car could race, and a few where they can't—in 1986, two 959 variants finished first and second in the famous Paris-Dakar Rally. The GT3 RS puts that racing heritage on the road.

**Above:** The engine of the 911 GT3 is bolted to the body via two separate mounts in an optional dynamic mount system developed for the car. Electronically controlled, its purpose is to reduce the vibration from the engine and drivetrain felt by the rest of the car.

**Left to right:** The car has a water-cooled six-cylinder boxer engine with four-valve cylinder heads. It revs to a maximum of 8,500 rpm and powers the car to 62 mph in just 4.1 seconds, with a top speed of 194 mph.

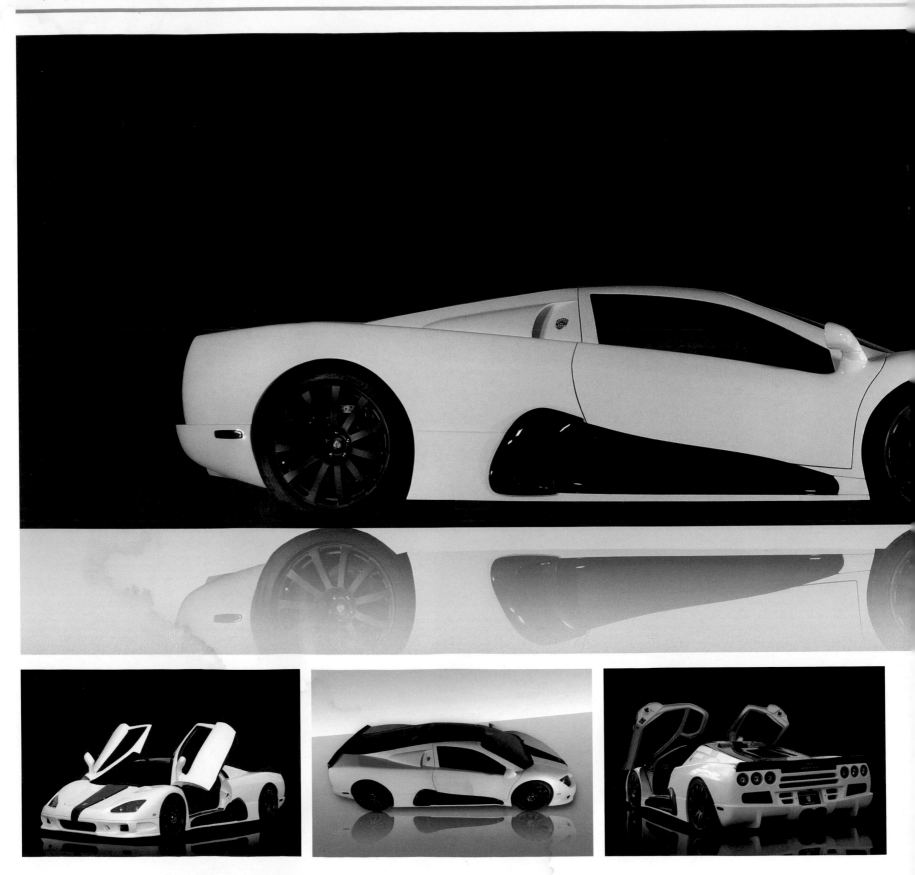

# Shelby SuperCars Ultimate Aero—The world's fastest car?

Of all the accolades and absolutes in the sports car world, one stands out. The undisputed, independently-verified title of world's fastest production car is the most sought-after, and changes very rarely. But in October 2007, a tiny American sports car maker called Shelby SuperCars, or SSC, took that title away from the mighty Bugatti Veyron, despite the hundreds of millions of dollars that parent company Volkswagen had poured into the Veyron project. Just as astonishingly the driver, Chuck Bigelow, was 71 years old when he broke the record on a 12-mile stretch of road not far from SSC's home. Though freshly paved, the course wasn't straight, with several elevation changes and an S-bend in the middle. Bigelow said that with a straighter road, the record would have been 'considerably higher'. But nobody was disappointed with the staggering 257 mph two-way average he recorded that day.

SSC began producing the Ultimate Aero in 2007, after years of development and some initial launch challenges. The company was founded by Jerod Shelby, who grew up in Richland, Washington, near the current SSC headquarters. He was a competitive kart racer as a boy and, after achieving success as an inventive medical equipment engineer, he set about turning his dream of building a world-class American supercar into reality in the late 1990s.

Several years later, a handful of standard Aeros had been produced. Rumors and discussion about the new Ultimate Aero, as well as a record attempt, came and went until SSC officially announced its intentions. The first attempt was made on a public road in northeast Nevada, near the Bonneville Salt Flats during early spring of 2007, but it was snowed out, although the car managed a 241 mile-per-hour run with veteran high-speed driver, Rick Doria, at the wheel. About six months later, Shelby saw the car that bears his name break the record and seize that title just prior his 40th birthday. A small sports car maker can't buy publicity like that. And the credibility that comes with the title can only be earned.

**Above:** The Ultimate Aero is made from carbon-fiber, composite, and a steel space frame, and is a mid-engine, rear drive design. It features forged, three-piece alloy wheels and Michelin Pilot Sport PS2 tires, with rack and pinion assisted steering.

**Left to right:** The engine is an SSC-designed billet aluminum V8 block, with a sequential, multi-port fuel injection induction system, twin turbochargers, and dual water-to-air intercoolers. The car has achieved a zero-to-60 time of 2.78 seconds.

# Spyker C8 LM85—The flying Dutchman of the road

*Nulla tenaci invia est via*: 'For the tenacious, no road is impassable.' It's a good slogan for a company and a great one for a racing team. Anyone observing this tiny company's forays into motorsport knows that Spyker struggled mightily, especially in endurance races. Yet its the determination to soldier on in the face of adversity that ultimately earned the company admiration, if not victories. And it earned it exposure, credibility, and vital engineering experience for their road cars, like the C8 LM85.

Spyker takes its inspiration from the Dutch company founded by brothers Jacobus and Hendrik-Jan Spijker in the late 1800s. Originally a coach company—the horse kind—they evolved into a car manufacturer, producing the world's first four-wheel drive car with a single engine and four-wheel brakes.

Known for their quality and rugged engineering, the cars were also successful in racing. They were taken over by an aviation company in 1914, when the propeller logo was introduced, and released a car called the C1. Thought the business centred around aircraft and aircraft engines, they released another car, the C4, noted for its engine designed by Wilhelm Maybach, before closing in 1926.

The name—and spirit of excellence—was revived when Victor Muller and Maarten de Bruijn founded Spyker Cars in 2000, with Muller as CEO until 2007. The Spyder convertible was unveiled that same year at the Birmingham Motor Show, with the Laviolette coupé arriving in 2001 at the Amsterdam Motor Show.

Spyker describes its cars as the 'ultimate statement of individuality: a creation of timeless beauty in the form of a state-of-the-art technology package with spectacular performance,' and as the brand approaches the decade mark, the motoring public are starting to show their approval with their wallets.

**Above:** The LM85 was designed to match the spirit of the Spyker Squadron GT2 (LMES) race team and features a livery inspired by the GT2. It is named after the starting number of the GT2 cars that have appeared at Le Mans since 2002.

**Left to right:** The LM85 is an advanced, mid-engine, two-seater sportscar, with an all-aluminum body and an Audi 4.2 Liter V8 engine that provides 400 bhp, and a manual six-speed Getrag gearbox.

## Tesla Roadster Sport—The "green" car that has others seeing red on the track

One hundred and fifty years to the month since the birth of electrical genius Nikola Tesla, the first all-electric sports car was launched in Santa Monica, California. It bore Tesla's name—and his AC induction motor technology—in tribute. Supported by a list of investors that reads like a who's who of the tech industry, the company had delivered nearly 150 production vehicles to eager buyers by the end of 2008. And the Sport model announced in early 2009 promised to improve further on performance that shocked—if you'll pardon the pun—the sports car establishment.

Unlike hybrids, which use both gasoline and electric power, the Tesla has only batteries and an electric motor and can travel up to 220 miles on a single charge. Several companies are working on electric-only technology, but only Tesla offers for general sale a production, eco-friendly electric sports car that can rocket to 60 miles per hour in a supercar-standard 3.7 seconds, and hit a top speed of 125 miles per hour.

Sports car fans will notice the resemblance of the Tesla to the Lotus Elise, as it was developed with the help of Lotus Cars in Norfolk, England. Their lightweight roadster lent its underpinnings to the Tesla, giving it a compact platform that was already a handling superstar.

Tesla asserts that electric-only cars offer the ultimate freedom, because they aren't dependent on any one energy source for power. Wind, solar, hydro, nuclear, coal, or even technologies yet to be discovered can be used to create the electricity that powers it, without changing its design. Even more exciting for drivers who crave a great driving experience is that the car's performance rivals that of many costing two to three times more, and it produces it with a complete absence of tailpipe emissions or environmental guilt.

**Above:** The Tesla Roadster Sport has no clutch pedal—one touch of a pedal is all that's required to get moving, without the sluggish response of an automatic. A favorite trick of the manufacturer is to invite the passenger to reach forward and turn on the radio and accelerate as they do so—so fast that he or she can't sit forward enough to reach the dials.

**Left to right:** Unlike a gasoline engine, which only reaches peak torque in a narrow rpm range, forcing frequent gear changes, the Tesla delivers full torque at all times, even when at a stand.

# TVR Sagaris—The aggressive battle axe that keeps rolling

If TVR ever decides to change its corporate name, a cat would be the most appropriate choice, as the United Kingdom-based carmaker seems to have at least nine lives. Started by Trevor Wilkinson just after World War II, like many sports car makers it takes its name from its founder. But TVR does it differently, taking its title from the consonants in Trevor's first name. Doing things differently has become a TVR trademark.

It manufactured high-performance kit cars that avoided tax until the regulations were changed in the 1970s. Through the years, it has made traditional British sports cars with long hoods and short cabins. The aggressive styling of modern TVRs helps the company differentiate its products from other sports cars in the marketplace. Quality and reliability have often been questioned, but the extraordinary looks, noise, and acceleration of TVRs give buyers a reason to pick them over the flawless but more common and less characterful Porsches and BMW you can have for the same price.

A sagaris is a type of battle axe typically found in ancient Persia, designed to chop through the armor of rival armies. Perhaps the naming of the Sagaris sports car was meant to suggest an ability to cut into sales of major rivals, which it has to do if the company is to survive. TVR has often been in the news in recent years as young Russian billionaire Nikolai Smolensky bought the company, managed it into bankruptcy, then bought it again as the highest bidder at auction.

The Sagaris was first shown shown in 2003, and was engineered from the ground up to be an endurance racecar that was legal for the streets. It went on sale in 2005, but TVR ceased production soon after. An updated Sagaris 2 was announced in the summer of 2008, with promises that the company would restart production in early 2009.

**Above:** The four-liter 380 bhp engine, also used in the Tuscan S, will run happily at low speeds in high gears, but excels when the pedal is put to the metal: the car reaches 60 mph in 3.7 seconds.

**Left to right:** The research team joined forces with Bilstein to desgin the suspension and handling, which combine with a rigid tubular steel rollcage and wider track to make the Sagaris both energizing and safe for the driver.

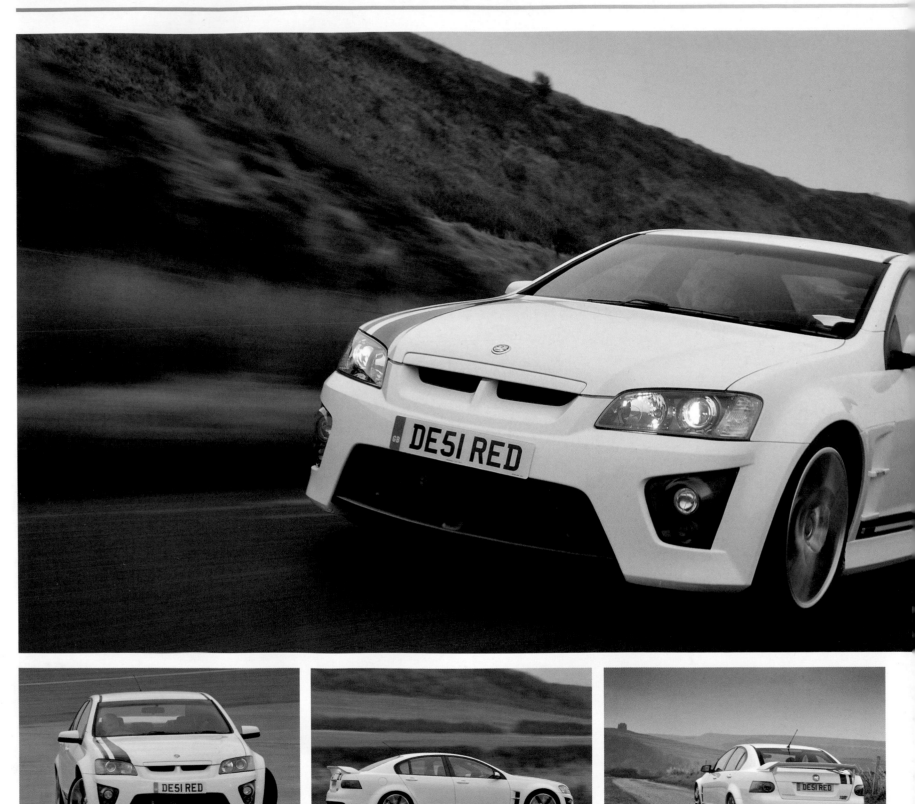

# Vauxhall VXR8—The wild Australian racer

Australia is a big country with a small but completely car-obsessed population. The cars it produces reflect this. To cope with the distances between major cities, they're big, spacious inside, and often run large-capacity V8 engines with tall gearing that will cruise lazily all day. But to satisfy petrolhead Aussie buyers, the two big local carmakers—Ford and Holden, the latter a subsidiary of General Motors—also produce an endless stream of in-house high-performance derivatives. They're affordable and sensational to drive, and fortunately interest in them shows no sign of slowing, despite Australia imposing speed limits on its last unrestricted roads, and tight limits, strict enforcement, and painful fines everywhere else.

Holden Special Vehicles, or HSV, is the firm's factory performance division and has produced some sensational road cars, as well some wild racers; Australian touring cars closely resemble the road versions of the big-selling Ford Falcon and Holden Commodore and provide some of the best racing action on the planet. The Bathurst 1,000 km race deserves recognition as one of the world's great motorsport events, alongside the Monaco Grand Prix, Le Mans, the Indy 500, and the Paris-Dakar rally.

For too long, Aussie cars stayed at home. But that's starting to change. GM's former product chief Bob Lutz—a  former fighter pilot and genuine car enthusiast—championed the work of GM's Aussie outpost. The Holden Monaro coupé was brought to the US as the Pontiac GTO, and HSV's take on the both the Monaro and the four-door Commodore were put on sale in Europe after desperate buyers started importing them themselves.

This Vauxhall VXR8 is the UK version of HSV Clubsport. It's sold in the US as the most extreme version of the Pontiac G8. And if you're wondering what a big, four-door car like this is doing in a collection of sports cars, you just need to drive one.

**Above:** The VXR8 halo model is a product of the Vauxhall commitment to improvement, carrying the spirit of its predecessors and enhanced with a V8 engine for added performance and power.

**Left to right:** The VXR8 is fitted with 19-inch ten-spoke alloy wheels and specially-developed Bridgestone tires, and the front and rear brake calipers carry the VXR logo. The car features LED "afterburner" tail lights and a rear bumper with twin diffusers. The MacPherson strut front suspension has progressive rate front springs.

# Vehicle Design

Oddly, for such a distinctively Australian car, the two men with the strongest influence on HSV's development are Scottish. Former racing driver and Formula 1 team owner Tom Walkinshaw established the HSV brand and ensures the cars' design and engineering are up to the standards that brought him Le Mans victories.

Fellow Scot Ian Callum, one of the world's most acclaimed car designers, was design director prior to joining Jaguar and established a muscular look for the cars that continues today.

Under the skin, HSVs aren't particularly complex. Their appeal, and their affordability, comes from sticking to simple principles. Lack of complexity means relatively light weight for a large car. A big, easily tuneable V8 gives big-hearted performance; the standard car gives 415 hp, and that can be increased to 530 hp with a factory supercharger kit.

Don't expect any fancy F1-style hydraulically-actuated, paddle-shift gearboxes; this is a car you drive yourself, so there's a sweet-shifting six-speed Tremec manual transmission. And, of course, power goes to the rear wheels only, because it just wouldn't be an Aussie car if you couldn't indulge in long, smoky powerslides.

**Top:** The car comes with a multi-function display panel and electronic climate control with variable side-to-side temperature settings.The seats are electrically adjustable and leather-covered.

**Middle:** Auxiliary gauges display the oil temperature, oil pressure, and battery voltage.

**Bottom:** The interior is fitted with Dakar leather and suede.

# Performance

Unlike cars that make it too easy for drivers, you'll need some skill to extract the maximum acceleration from a VXR8, balancing revs and clutch to get just the right mount of wheelspin off the line. But doing it yourself and getting it right is so much more satisfying. Nail it and you'll produce a 0-60mph time of just 4.8 seconds, a match for many European exotics, and on those long, straight Australian highways the VXR8 will charge on to an unrestricted 175mph, if the cops don't catch you first.

The soundtrack is pure rolling thunder, and you can turn the volume up to 11 with a factory "loud kit" for the exhaust. Handling is remarkably agile for such a big car; HSV puts as much effort into how its cars corner as how hard they go, and it shows.

## At a Glance

**Country of manufacture**
Australia

**Engine**
Front-mounted, General Motors LS3 V8 with aluminum alloy block and heads.

| | |
|---|---|
| Displacement | 6.2 liter |
| Horsepower | 425 @ 6,000 rpm |
| Torque | 405 lb-ft @ 4,500 rpm |

**Drivetrain**
6-speed manual transmission (6-speed auto optional) sending power to the rear wheels.

**Suspension, handling, & braking**
Independent 4-wheel suspension, stability and traction control systems, vented anti-lock disc brakes front and rear with 4-caliper front calipers and 2-piston rear calipers, all in red.

**Weights and measurements**

| | |
|---|---|
| Curb weight | 4,036 lbs |
| Length | 194.5 in |
| Width | 85.6 in |
| Height | 57.8 in |

**Performance**

| | |
|---|---|
| 0–60 mph (mfr est.) | 4.9 sec |
| Top speed (mfr est.) | 155 mph (electronically limited) |

**Trivia**
The previous generation Commodore chassis was exported to the United States as the Pontiac GTO.

# Virago Coupé—Stature and strength from the femme fatale

Perhaps more than any other car in this collection, the new Virago Coupé encapsulates what a good sports car should be. It doesn't have to be ludicrously powerful. It doesn't have to be forbiddingly expensive. It doesn't have to be awkward to get into, scary to drive, or hard to see out of. It just needs to look great and be fun to drive; nothing more.

Plenty of sports cars manage that. But most are produced in big numbers, and some buyers want a sports car with some rarity, produced in sufficiently low volumes to allow them to get to know the people who make it, visit the factory as their car is being assembled, and put their own personal stamp on it.

The United Kingdom has more small sports car makers than any other country. Low volumes and high development costs make it a risky business. Many start, and only a handful survive. But the omens for Virago are very good indeed. It has a great-looking car, designed and engineered in such a way that a small firm can produce it to the high standards buyers demand. It targets an interesting gap in the market. And the people behind it aren't exactly car industry novices.

'Creating and building this car is a great opportunity and a dream job, but I have spent enough time in business to be hard-headed about it,' said Andy Nowson, Virago's Managing Director, who came to the project from a senior executive position at Land Rover.

'Virago is not aimed at the "ultimate-power" buyer, but rather at those looking for a stunning, reliable, practical, yet fast and fun, daily sports coupé,' he explains.

That's an appealing combination of attributes; add in exclusivity and affordability, and Nowson and his team are set for success.

**Above:** The Virago team of designers, engineers, and drivers have worked for major manufacturers and F1 teams, combining their expertise and experience to create a car that thinks only of its driver.

**Left to right:** The car was designed to be the ultimate day car, and the ultimate weekend car too, with sleek lines and an emphasis on charisma from every angle.

# Wiesmann GT MF4-S—A fusion of form and function

You might not have heard of Wiesmann. If you live in the United States, you have a good excuse, as this tiny German sports car maker doesn't yet offer its cars for sale in America. But here are a couple of small but significant facts to get you started. First, for years, Wiesmann was the only carmaker to which BMW would supply engines made by its elite M division. BMW simply wouldn't risk its reputation by allowing its engines to appear in another company's car, unless it thought those cars were pretty special to drive, and engineered and built to the same or higher standards than BMWs. What do many M-division engineers keep in their garage for weekends, when they're done creating some of the world's best sports cars? A Wiesmann.

And here's another impressive endorsement. If you're in the market for a Bugatti Veyron, the company will fly in a French former Formula 1 driver to accompany you on the world's best test drive. His name is Pierre-Henri Raphanel. And while his day job might be driving the world's most expensive car, at home he has a Wiesmann.

Founded in 1985 by brothers Martin and Friedhelm Wiesmann, the company fashions roadsters and coupés that are rolling artwork. The pair started out making hardtops for convertibles, then rolled out their first car, a roadster, in 1993. The car was built around a galvanized steel chassis equipped with BMW running gear. This gave them complete freedom in design, but the performance and reliability of an established drivetrain.

The GT MF4-S is the coupé derivative of the roadster. It was unveiled at the 2003 Frankfurt Auto Show, and a race version was campaigned in the arduous Nürburgring 24-hour race. It is fitted with BMW's sensational 4.8-liter V8 from the new M3.

**Above:** The engine is a BMW six-cylinder in-line motor with 343 hp; maximum torque is 4,900 rpm. The car has a five-gear manual transmission with a six-gear available, or six-gear sequential.

**Left to right:** The body of the car is high quality, fiberglass-reinforced composite material. The front axel has a McPherson strut with control arm and stabilizer, and a multi-link rear axle with transverse and longitudinal control arm and stabilizer. The GT MF4-S is a rear-wheel drive.

# Zenvo ST1—The great Dane

Where do you start with the Zenvo ST1? With the fact this it is Denmark's first and only supercar? With its extreme, angular, ground-breaking looks? With its equally extreme power and torque figures, both of which are in four figures? With the fact that its top speed has to be electronically limited to 233 mph, at which speed it will cross its home country in just 18 minutes? Whichever way you look at it, the ST1 is a staggering new sportscar from a brand—and indeed a country—with no automotive heritage. But it looks set to give the established players a real shock.

A decade in the making, the car was given the go-ahead in 2005 and rough sketches were made the following year. The design of the prototype was approved in early 2008, with dynamometer, initial drive, and performance test runs coming later in the year. Only when the company was sure the car was exactly what it envisioned were photos of the prototype released to the public in late 2008.

Zenvo's Nordic logo incorporates a shield with the name at the top and a stylized drawing of Thor's hammer, intended to represent 'massive cars with plenty of strength'. There are varying reports on the source of the name—one being that it was created by combining the last names of co-founders, Jesper Jensen and Troels Vollertsen. Though the pair intentionally set out to create an over-the-top supercar, they have been reluctant to say too much about their project to ensure they didn't promise something they couldn't deliver.

'We realized that Denmark had no design or engineering heritage in this field,' Jensen told Denmark's *Bilmagasinet* magazine, 'Which was why we didn't reveal anything at all until we were 100 percent ready. We didn't want to make promises we could not keep. Even some of our suppliers and partners were cynical to begin with.'

Zenvo leadership wanted to create a car with extreme exclusivity, and felt that producing hundreds of units would dilute its significance. Hence just 15 units are scheduled for production.

**Above:** The power of the Zenvo ST1 comes from its seven-liter V8 engine, which has both a turbo and supercharger, developing 1,104 bhp of power amd 1,430 nm of torque.

**Left to right:** Touted as the first fully Danish design, making use of the cutting edge designers from Denmark, the car has carbon-fiber body panels, polished stainless steel exhaust outlets, and a racing light steel frame structure. The Xenon headlamps, light-tinted glass and metallic paint complete the look.

# Acknowledgements

The publishers would like to thank the following for their kind permission to use their pictures and illustrations:

Alfa Romeo

Ascari (courtesy of Steven Nesta)

Aston Martin

Audi

Bentley

BMW

Bolwell

Breckland

Bugatti

Chevrolet

Chrysler

Ferrari

Ford

Gumpert

Honda

Jaguar

Koenigsegg

Automobili Lamborghini. S.p.A.

Lexus

Lotus

Maserati

Mercedes-Benz

Mosler

Nissan (GTR pictures courtesy of Dom Fraser)

Pagani

Panoz

Porsche

Shelby SuperCars

Spyker

Tesla Motors, Inc.

Vauxhall

Virago

Wiesmann

Zenvo

## Picture Credits

Alamy p18-21 (all), p56 (top)

Kimball Images p46-47 (all), p48 (top)

Getty Images p48 (middle, bottom), p16-19 (all)

Corbis p49 (middle), p54 (all), p56 (middle, bottom), p57 (bottom), p106-109 (all)

The publishers wish to thank Tim Pollard and the team at *Car Magazine* for their involvement.